THE CREATIVE JOURNAL
FOR TEENS

OTHER WORKS BY DR. LUCIA CAPACCHIONE

Books
The Creative Journal: The Art of Finding Yourself
The Creative Journal for Children
The Creative Journal for Parents
The Power of Your Other Hand
Recovery of Your Inner Child
Visioning: Ten Steps to Designing the Life of Your Dreams
Putting Your Talent to Work (with Peggy Van Pelt)
The Well-Being Journal
Lighten Up Your Body, Lighten Up Your Life (with Johnson and Strohecker)
The Picture of Health: Healing Your Life with Art
Living with Feeling: The Art of Emotional Expression

Tapes
The Wisdom of Your Other Hand (5 tapes on The Creative Journal and art therapy, inner family work, body/mind healing, relationships and career) Sounds True
The Picture of Health Audio Tape (Guided Meditation/Journaling)
The Sound of Feelings (set of 5 tapes or CDs) music by Jessie Allen Cooper with Lucia Capacchione narrating

For information regarding materials, public presentations, consulting, or the Creative Journal Expressive Arts certification training program, contact:

Lucia Capacchione
P.O. Box 1355
Cambria, CA 93428
(805) 546-1424
Web site: www.luciac.com

THE CREATIVE JOURNAL FOR TEENS
Second Edition

Making Friends with Yourself

By
Lucia Capaccione, Ph.D.

New Page Books
A division of The Career Press, Inc.
Franklin Lakes, NJ

THE CREATIVE JOURNAL FOR TEENS: SECOND EDITION
Typeset by B. Rosen
Cover design by Lu Rossman/Digi Dog Design
Printed in the U.S.A. by Book-mart Press

To order this title, please call toll-free 1-800-CAREER-1 (NJ and Canada: 201-848-0310) to order using VISA or MasterCard, or for further information on books from Career Press.

The Career Press, Inc., 3 Tice Road, PO Box 687
Franklin Lakes, NJ 07417
www.careerpress.com
www.newpagebooks.com

Library of Congress Cataloging-in-Publication Data
Capacchione, Lucia.
   Creative journal for teens : making friends with yourself / by Lucia Capacchione.--2nd ed.
      p. cm.
   Includes bibliographical references (p.).
   ISBN 1-56414-572-7 (pbk.)
      1. English language--Composition and exercises--Study and teaching. 2. Diaries--Authorship. 3. Self-perception in adolescence. 4. Creative ability in Adolescence. I. Title.

LB15676 .C3164 2001
808'.06692--dc21

                                                    2001044270

*Dedicated to
teenage diarists*
ANNE FRANK
and
ANAÏS NIN
*for their inspiration and guidance and
to my daughters,* CELIA *and* ALETA,
*for their invaluable help
in developing this book.*

THANKS

To my editor, Francesca Nemko, for her patience and tireless work in assisting me to complete this book for publication.

To Ann Tidwell of Venice High School, Venice, Florida and Ruth Stanton of Hoover High School, Glendale, California for using this manuscript with their students and gathering examples of journal work

To all the young people who so generously shared their drawings and writings as illustrations. Without their wonderful journal work, this book would not have been possible. Their names are:

Don Badalamenti	Sean Holbert	Mike Rafavielle
Brian J. Birch	Jay Heldebrandt	Ileana Rivera
Jim Butler	Adrine Khachatrian	Kim Sangster
John Creasy	Jason King	Raed Shehead
Rob Eddy	Lynne LeVesque	Sabrina Stella
Jeff Fulcher	Brad Lugar	Jennifer Standridge
James Given	Richard Martin	Jennifer Svendsen
Jason Gomez	Cher McBrayer	Michelle Wachelka
Julie Grafil	Jenny McClain	Noel West
Racquel Claudia Grant	Martin M'Guire	Mike Williams
Missi Groves	Curtis Myers	Ben Wood
Jesse Gura	Heather O'Brien	Eric Woods
Kevin Hanley	Amanda Oster	Chen Yu
Glenis Harps	Celia Pearce	

And thanks to:
My publisher, Ron Fry, for his continued support, and the designers, for their fine presentation of this book.

Contents

CHAPTER ONE

Beginnings

When I was a little girl, my mother had a book that fascinated me. Bound in brown alligator skin with gold edging on the pages, it had the word *Diary* embossed in gold on the cover. There was a leather flap from the back cover to the front that kept the book secured shut with a shiny gold lock. My mother never locked her diary, however, for she never wrote in it. There were no secrets inside, only a tiny gold key in a little paper envelope. There were no words written on its neatly lined pages.

I loved that little empty diary, and enjoyed thumbing through its blank pages. Maybe it was its antique appearance that appealed to me—the bumpy leather binding, the richness of the gold edged pages, the shininess of the miniature lock and key. The book was so fancy that I couldn't imagine anyone actually writing in it. Also, there was something wonderful and mysterious about the blankness of the book: It was full of possibilities.

Then one day I was given a diary of my own. It wasn't as fancy as my mother's (it had a royal blue imitation leather cover), so I felt OK about writing in it. It was like my mom's in every other way, though, right down to the flap, the gold lock and key, and the word *Diary* in gold on the cover. I was delighted with it.

At first, it was fun. Faithfully, I made an entry each day. "Dear Diary, Today I..." and then "...happened." And so it went. But after a while, I felt cramped by the small space provided for each day's entry. So much more to say, so little room to say it. Then, after a while, I grew bored with chronicling events and gradually stopped making entries in my dear diary altogether.

However, I didn't stop writing. At school, I wrote well and with great enthusiasm. My teachers were pleased and encouraged me. More importantly, I continued writing for myself. Every now and then I would pick up a steno pad that I kept in my closet and write about something important to me: my teacher at art school, the painters I admired, my own painting, and my feelings about art. I loved doing this kind of personal writing so much, I'm surprised I didn't do it more often.

At fifteen, I won second prize in our local newspaper's essay contest on the theme of "future career." I wrote about wanting to become a journalist. We had to collect our prizes at the local variety store and, while I was waiting in line, a little blank book in the stationery department caught my eye. It was a black and red hardbound ledger-type book with the word *Record* neatly embossed in gold on the cover. The pages were blank except for the lines. I reasoned that because I was going to be a journalist, I'd need a very special notebook in which to write. I thought, "I might even write a book someday." So I bought it.

But I put the book away and promptly forgot about it and about becoming a journalist. Painting became my great love. Upon graduating from high school, I went to college as an art major and English minor. After becoming a professional artist, marriage followed, then the birth of two daughters. A career change came next, which led to teaching young children and supervising Head Start programs in the inner city of Los Angeles. The years passed.

Then during a serious illness when I was thirty-five, I found the little record book I had purchased twenty years earlier. From my sick bed I noticed it on a nearby shelf. It had stayed with me through all kinds of changes, moves, and even a divorce. It was still blank but something told me to write my deepest feelings and thoughts, my pain and fear, my wishes and dreams, the words of my inner world. This was my first "official" journal. And the process of journal-keeping through writing and drawing helped heal me from a mysterious illness that had defied the doctors and their medicines.

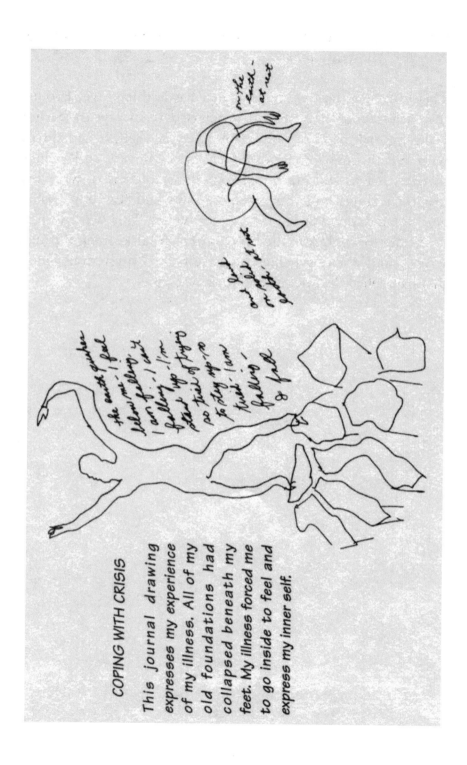

COPING WITH CRISIS

This journal drawing expresses my experience of my illness. All of my old foundations had collapsed beneath my feet. My illness forced me to go inside to feel and express my inner self.

Today I feel STUCK
STUCK
STUCK IN A HOLE

NOT MOVING · NOT KNOWING·
WHERE OR HOW TO FLOW·····?
FREEDOM FRIGHTENS ME.
I CAN DO WHATEVER I WANT
I CAN CREATE MY OWN GARDEN
I CAN CREATE SOMETHING IS STILL
BUT SOMETHING IS STILL
STOPPING ME·
KEEPING ME TIED DOWN·

Looking inside was not always easy. I had to face feelings of fear, frustration, loneliness, and anger, but it was worth it, because I found myself.

Treasure the chaos out of which order emerges.
Cherish the puzzlement leading to the light.
Deep inside this nest is the self to be found.

How can I speak my joy in words? I can't remain within the boundaries of nouns and verbs . . . so I flow into the poetry of words and pictures, of song and sound, of movement . . . the singing of my body, the gestures of my soul. Hold me earth and sea, take me up wind and clouds. Hold me in your arms—I am floating away.

The sense of freedom and joy I experienced through my healing was like nothing I had ever known before.

My life changed so much after that. I began listening to my own feelings and inner wisdom. The insights I gained through journal-keeping led me into a new career as an art therapist and teacher of diary writing and drawing. I call my method The Creative Journal. But more importantly, I learned to play and enjoy life again. For instance, at thirty-nine, I started skateboarding for the first time in my life and loved it.

Photo by Jim Ruebsamen, Santa Monica Evening Outlook.

Skateboarding at Venice Beach, California.

At fifteen, I had no way of consciously knowing where that little record book would lead me. How could I have known that I would carry it around among my possessions for twenty years before writing a word in it? How could I have known that instead of a journalist's notebook, it would become the first volume of many personal journals that have been my laboratory for developing the many books I have authored?

In looking back, it is clear that at age fifteen I intuitively knew more than I thought. I had set a dream in motion and, although it went underground for twenty years, that dream and the little blank book that was its symbol came back at the time when I needed them most. My girlhood vision came true, although not in the form that I expected. I became a "journalist" after all: a journalist of the inner world. And I'm grateful to that fifteen-year-old girl that I was for having the sense to buy a little blank book. I used it to save my life and to help others.

WHAT IS CREATIVE JOURNAL-KEEPING?

Creative journal-keeping is a tool for understanding yourself better. It can also help you develop skill in writing and in drawing. The method consists of *simple exercises* to be done in a diary or personal journal. The exercises are designed to help you:

- express feelings and thoughts.
- feel comfortable writing and drawing.
- acquire a habit of self-expression.
- communicate in words and pictures.
- become more observant.
- know and like yourself better.
- appreciate your experiences more.
- use imagination and natural talents.
- strengthen concentration and focus.

- enjoy self-reflection through words and pictures.
- solve problems and be more self-reliant.
- find your own wisdom inside.

The exercises are arranged in a particular order from simple to more complex. The Table of Contents lists the exercises by name so that you can easily locate the ones you wish to do. If you are using this book under the guidance of an adult (teacher, counselor, parent, etc.) you may be assigned specific exercises. If you are using this book on your own, first read through the book so that you know what it is and how it works. Become familiar with the exercises before doing them. When you start journal-keeping, begin at the beginning and go through each chapter in the order given. Later on you can reuse the book by choosing the exercise that appeals to you at the time. Do what feels right for you. I trust you to know what you need and to follow your own common sense. Use it creatively and playfully.

- Change or expand the exercises if you wish.
  (There's room in the book for your additions
  and notes.)
- Use journal ideas from other sources.
- Invent your own journal exercises on the pages provided at the end of each chapter.

FORMS OF EXPRESSION: WORDS AND PICTURES

Diaries and journals are usually thought of as written records of personal experiences, thoughts, and feelings. The creative journal is different. It includes art as well as writing. There are many ways to express what is inside you:

- scribbles, doodles, and drawings.
- graphs and diagrams.

- colors and abstract designs.
- symbols.
- representational sketches.

If you don't like to write or don't think you can write very well, the art activities in this book may help you get interested in keeping a journal. Lots of times it's much easier and more fun to draw *first*. Drawing is a good way to warm up. Words often flow after a picture has been drawn.

If you think you don't have any talent in art, drawing privately in your journal will help you get over being self-conscious. No one is going to see your journal drawings (or your writings) unless you show them. So you don't have to worry about being laughed at or criticized or given a "bad grade." There are no grades for what you write or draw in your journal. So when you write, hopefully you can relax and experiment with:

- writing in free association, stream of consciousness ("free-write").
- prose and poetry.
- dramatic dialogues (play scripting).
- description.
- autobiographical stories.

Privacy is a very important part of creative journal-keeping. Your journal belongs to you. If it is not private, then you will probably not have the freedom to really be yourself. And if you can't be honest with yourself in your journal, there's no point in using this method.

The purpose of creative journal-keeping is to understand your self better. This happens through free expression of thoughts, feelings, and experiences. It is often hard to be honest if you are in danger of being criticized by others. By removing the reactions of other people altogether, confidential journal-keeping lets you be truthful with yourself. Diaries and journals have always been private. That's why they had locks on them. A diary has always been a place "to tell it like it is," a place to dream and wish, to brainstorm creative ideas, to share your innermost self with yourself.

Anne Frank's teenage diary became famous after she was killed by the Nazis during World War II. Here is what she wrote in her first diary entry:

> I hope I shall be able to confide in you completely, as I have never been able to do in anyone before, and I hope that you will be a great support and comfort to me.

It was her thirteenth birthday and the beginning of a diary that was to become world-famous as a book, a play, and a movie. Another diary entry of Anne's says a lot about how she used her diary and how much she valued the privacy it gave her:

> I have two things to confess to you today, which will take a long time. But I must tell someone and you are the best one to tell, as I know that, come what may, you always keep a secret.

Everyone I know who keeps a journal for self-understanding has reported that the privacy has given him or her the freedom to "get things off my chest," as they say. There is a great relief if one is holding in strong feelings. Anne Frank said it clearly in her diary:

> I can shake off everything if I write; my sorrows disappear, my courage is reborn....

TALENT AND CREATIVITY: WE'VE ALL GOT IT

All human beings are creative and expressive. Unfortunately, in our culture, most people think they are untalented when it comes to art or writing or both. How many times have you heard or said, "I can't draw a straight line," or "I'm just not artistic," or "I was born with no talent"?

These are learned beliefs. They usually result from criticism of our early childhood attempts to express ourselves. Someone ridiculed our drawing or writing and so we concluded that we couldn't do it. That excused us from even trying. First, you buy the idea that you don't have "it" then you can't possibly use "it." Right? *Wrong.* This is distorted logic based on the mistaken belief that only a few people have talent and the rest of us don't. Certainly there are some people with perception problems and physical handicaps, but the truth is that many people can't draw or write because *they think they can't* and because they *never or rarely do it.* It's as simple as that.

Most people have had little or no encouragement, training, or opportunity in art. They may have had unhappy experiences. In the case of writing, they may have received formal instruction in school, but it was always attached to grades and judgment. They didn't write for their own enjoyment and creative growth.

The Creative Journal approaches things differently. It's a safe method for testing the waters of self-expression. *You will have the freedom to try new things, to have fun with words and pictures, to discover abilities you didn't even know you had.* Other young people who are keeping creative journals are finding great value in it. Some even develop a fond attachment to their "dear diary." They report that it's a place to express who they really are. One twelve year old girl who kept a journal regularly as part of a school program wrote:

Dear Journal:

Today is my first time I had you. I think you're a nice journal to be with. I hope to have you for ever and ever. I'm going to tell you lots of things about me. I like you a lot and thank the people that gave us the money to get you....

Carmen Melendez, the girl who wrote those words, later appeared on television and told about how much she had gained from journal-keeping on a regular basis. She was willing to share some of her journal voluntarily because she benefited so much from it.

USES OF CREATIVE JOURNAL-KEEPING

There are lots of situations and settings in which journaling can help you: at home, at school, while traveling, while hospitalized.

In Times of Trouble

Journal work is especially useful during difficult times, such as the following:

- family crisis.
- relocation.
- divorce or separation.
- school, classes, grade changes.
- illness or injury.
- addition of a new family member.
- death or illness of a loved one.
- conflict with others.
- job changes.

These events are often accompanied by strong feelings, such as:

- physical or emotional pain.
- confusion.
- insecurity.
- anger.
- fear.
- sadness or grief.

At such times, the journal can be a "good friend," a place to express difficult feelings. Sometimes it is hard to put these feelings into words, so drawing, doodling, or even scribbling can be a perfect way to let them out. At other times, the words may be there inside, but there is no one to tell them to. So the journal "listens" and "takes it all in" without judging or blaming you or saying, "Don't feel this," or "You shouldn't say that." You get to express your real feelings.

GUIDELINES FOR CREATIVE JOURNAL-KEEPING

Exercise Format

This book contains a series of exercises to be done in your own journal or blank book. Each exercise has its own title and guidelines.

Read each exercise over before doing it. Most of the exercises are divided into sections. *Do each subsection in the order in which it appears before going on.* If you try to do the entire exercise at once or do it out of order, you will probably get confused. Also, some of the exercises are too long to do at one sitting. You'll need more time. So for longer exercises, just do one or two subsections at a time.

Setting

Journaling is best done in a quiet setting. If done at home, a comfortable and private place is best. You should be free from interruptions and distractions. If you're doing journal work in a classroom or library, you should have a quiet atmosphere. It is best to have a short period of silence before you begin, so that you can focus your attention on what you are going to do in your journal.

Time

Journaling on a regular basis is a good way to acquire the habit and the skill. It need not be something you do every day. However, the more often you use your journal, especially in the beginning, the more benefits you will receive. Find the time of day that's best for you.

A ten to thirty minute session is recommended. Less than ten minutes is usually not enough time to really express what's on your mind. Be your own judge about how much time you need. It will depend upon what you have to write or draw. Sometimes you may use your journal more than once in the same day.

If you are doing journal work as part of a class in school or in counseling, a set time period will probably be assigned by your teacher or counselor. If you need more time, discuss this with the adult in charge and see if you can work out something that feels comfortable for you both.

Spontaneity

Use each exercise as a springboard to spark creativity and free expression. These exercises are not sacred. If you want to change an exercise, that is all to the good. Don't limit yourself. Use your imagination. You may find that certain exercises become your favorites. By all means go back to them as often as you like. Once you've done all the exercises in order, feel free to use them in any order you wish. Be creative.

Honesty

In order to understand yourself, it is necessary that you be honest with yourself. The journal is a place to really be yourself, feel your true feelings, and express them. That's why privacy is so important. If you are hiding from someone else's negative reaction, you won't be able to write and draw how you really feel. So keep your work confidential.

Privacy

Your journal is personal, private, and confidential. You have a right to privacy. You don't have to share your journal work or show it to anyone if you don't want to.

In order to protect your privacy, I suggest you keep your journal in a safe, private place: your desk, cabinet, carrying bag, or closet. Tell the people you live with or study with that the journal is private. If you think they won't respect your rights, then you might want to find a safe place to keep it. Whatever you do, make your journal confidential. It's private property and nobody else's business, unless you want to share something with them. It's your choice.

Selective Sharing

You may want to share a particular journal entry with a good friend, a teacher, or counselor that you trust. When I say someone you trust, I mean someone who accepts you the way you are, who doesn't criticize you, ridicule you, or put you down.

The purpose of this kind of journaling is to learn to understand and like yourself better. If you're around people who criticize you a lot, it's hard to like yourself. Hopefully, through creative journaling, you'll learn to appreciate yourself even when others don't. Critical people are not likely to understand you or your journal so I suggest that you do not share your journal with them. Remember, your journal is personal and needs to be protected from the critical attitudes of others.

MATERIALS FOR CREATIVE JOURNAL-KEEPING

A. **Notebook** with sturdy binding, 8 1/2" x 11" or 6" x 9". The best is a hardbound blank book with white, unlined paper. These are available at art supply or stationery stores and some bookstores. Spiral bound sketch pads are also good as long as they have unlined paper. A three-ring folder is also suitable, with unlined paper.

B. **Colored** felt pens in a set of eight or more colors. Medium or fine point pens can be used for both writing and drawing. You can also use *fat markers* or *crayons* for drawing. A regular pen or pencil or colored pencils can also be used. The reason for using color is that it helps express feelings more effectively. Color is more fun, too!

PREPARING TO WORK IN YOUR JOURNAL

When you are ready to do some journaling, choose a time and gather your materials (blank book and writing/drawing tools). Then find the right place: a spot that feels comfortable for you.

Be quiet and relax for a few minutes. You can close your eyes and take in some good, deep breaths.

Check out the feelings inside your body. Start with your head and face, then move down through each body part. Focus your attention and tune in to your body. Check out your torso, arms, and legs to see if there's any tension or pain in any area. Your body will really appreciate the time you are spending finding out what's happening.

If you find any tension or pain, just name that part of your body in your mind and let it relax. When you feel relaxed, slowly open your eyes. Now you are ready to start journaling.

The first thing to do each time you start journal work is to write the date on the first page of that day's entry. You don't need to date every page. You only want a record of each day's work so that you will be able to go back and see how your experiences unfold day by day. You'll probably notice changes and growth and you'll learn from your own personal history and experience.

Before you do any work remember: *Don't criticize your writing or your drawing.* Don't worry about grammar, spelling, or penmanship. This is just for you, so let yourself express thoughts and feelings without having to meet anybody else's demands. This is your life; this is your journal. Enjoy it!

CHAPTER TWO

What's Happening?

You are a unique human being. There has never been anyone exactly like you and there never will be. These exercises can help you look at what's going on at this time in your
life—moment by moment, day by day, week by week. You'll
be drawing and writing your own feelings, thoughts, and
experiences.

There are also examples from the journals of other young people like yourself. However, don't think you have to draw or
write the way they do. Remember, no one is giving you a
grade. No one is going to compare your work to anyone else's.
Your journal is for your eyes only, so have fun being yourself.

---

*"I must admit that only when I began to keep a
diary that my ideas began to take shape and pour
forth. To whom could I have confided all the
thoughts that fill my mind if not to a diary?"*

—Anaïs Nin, *Linotte: The Early Diary
of Anaïs Nin, 1914-1920*

OFF THE TOP OF MY HEAD

Choose a color and scribble or doodle any forms or designs on the page. You may want to use more than one page. Don't worry about making a "pretty picture" or anything recognizable. This isn't an art assignment. It's more like the kind of doodling people do when talking on the phone.

Write down any thoughts or feelings that float to the surface of your mind. Write quickly without pausing to think, evaluate, or criticize. You don't even have to form sentences. Don't worry about grammar, spelling, or punctuation. Just let the words flow onto the paper.

Choose a word from what you just wrote and write a paragraph. Write all your feelings and thoughts about that word. Again, do not worry about grammar, spelling, punctuation, or penmanship. Just let your feelings and thoughts come out.

"I really ought not to write this...but still, whatever you think of me, I can't keep everything to myself..."

—Anne Frank, *Diary of a Young Girl*

OFF THE TOP OF MY HEAD

One girl chose to write about love.

LOVE

Love is a special
word.
A word not to take
for granted.
Everybody loves
someone.
Whether it's your
mom, dad, dog, cat.
So tell someone
you love them.

FEELINGS

Be very quiet and "listen" to yourself. What emotions are you feeling right now? How do you feel physically?

Now draw a picture of how you feel right now. Doodle, scribble, or draw shapes, colors, pictures, or abstract designs. When you've finished your drawing, write about the feelings in *your drawing*.

Write a paragraph or more about how you feel right now.

Write a poem about a feeling. The poem doesn't have to rhyme, but it can. If you can't think of a feeling, here are some: sad, angry, happy, excited, nervous, afraid, lonely, frustrated, proud, playful, creative, hurt, depressed, enthusiastic. Illustrate your "feelings" poem with a picture.

"I'm boiling with rage...I'd like to stamp my feet, scream, give Mommy a good shaking, cry, and I don't know what else...But still, the brightest spot of all is that at least I can write down my thoughts and feelings, otherwise I would be absolutely stifled!"

—Anne Frank, *Diary of a Young Girl*

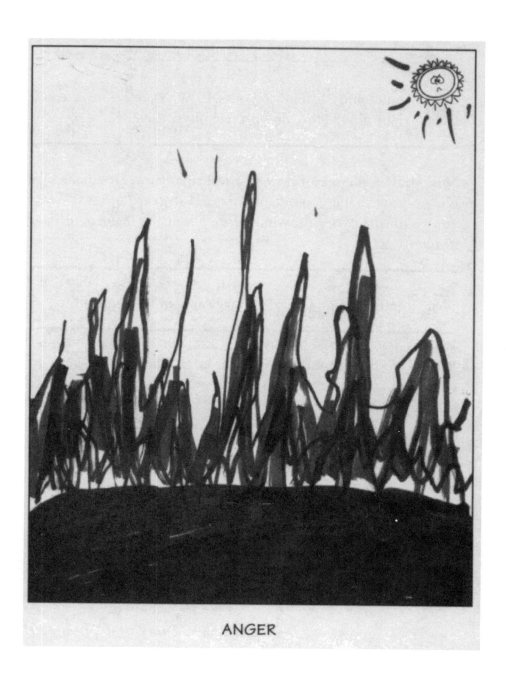

ANGER

HAPPINESS

Happiness is the feeling of security,
It's like when you're down & feeling sad,
when someone like Steve can really cheer you up.
Happiness is the feeling of security.
It's when friends are there for you,
in good times and bad.
Happiness is the feeling of security.

Sad
Guilt
Sorrow
Lonely
Hopeless
Wishful
Pitiful
Discreet
Quiet
Hurt

Depression is
love and sadness
caught in the middle
which explains a lot
of words: guilt, sorrow,
lonely, hopeless, and
wishful, but also pitiful,
discreet, quiet, & hurt.

I feel sad right now. I was and still am in love with a girl and
she broke up with me. That is why I feel like these words.

Anger:	I'm so sick of S. being pissed off at everything. Especially little things.
Me:	Why do I put up with it all the time?
Anger:	Because I know that I love him very much.
Me:	What should I do with all the anger that is built up inside me?
Anger:	Just don't hold it in. You've got to let it out somehow.
Me:	But how?
Anger:	That we have to work on.

I'm feeling lonely and afraid. I have friends, yes, but there are things you can't tell them. They see me every day at school and we talk but it's not really me there. I have no boyfriend to call my own because of how shy I am and distant.

Today I daydreamed again of me and my different self. I feel more comfortable in my dreams than I do in real life.

I'm so alone inside, but I pretend as if everything is fine on the outside. I need someone who does understand me and what I'm saying. I have that someone, but she's miles away at home. So I need someone here, close to me.

With people (friends) around me I can act like everything is fine, but when I'm alone the tears just fall, because then I face the fact that I'm really lonely in an unusual way. I hope you do understand me.

TODAY

Write a review of the day. Start with getting up this morning. Describe in detail the environments you were in, objects, colors, odors, sounds. Tell about the people you were with. Describe highlights of what happened, what you did, and how you felt.

What was the strongest feeling you had today? Perhaps you are still feeling it. Draw a picture of the feeling. Then write a conversation with the feeling as if you were writing the script for a play.

Write about something that's coming up in your life right now, and express your feelings about it.

**happy   excited   feel good   good day
Mom coming home   good weekend
have fun tomorrow   lot to do**

I am happy because I have not seen my mom in two months and tonight I get to see her.

WHERE I'M AT

Write about what's going on in your life at this time. How do you feel about it? Then draw a picture to express what you wrote about.

List things that are most important to you: people, objects, places, situations.

Describe a typical day in your life. Write about your routine: where you go, what you do, who you're with, clothes you wear, your interests.

Draw a big circle and diagram a typical week. Divide your circle into pie-shaped pieces, each representing a different part of your life: time with family, friends, school activities, sports, hobbies, time at work or doing household jobs, time at church or involved with community activities, time sleeping, etc. Each piece will be a different size depending on how much time you spend in any activity or place. Label each piece or do a drawing in each. (See example on next page by a girl in one of my journal classes.)

After drawing your diagram, write down your reactions. Are you happy with your use of time? Is there anything you'd change? How? Anything you can't change? How can you learn to accept that?

WHERE I'M AT

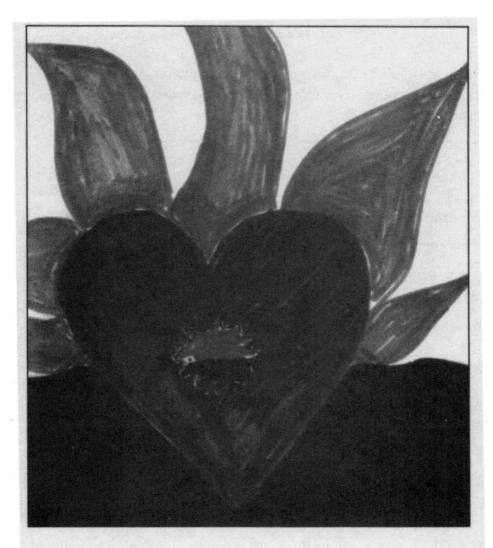

This is ridiculous. I'm going through another cycle of heartaches. I thought I was all over Bill but that empty feeling keeps returning. It's like a lump in my throat only the lump got lost and is in my heart. Once school gets going I'll be fine, but for the time being I hurt. It's so strange—I love him but know it'd never work again cause of my weird moods. I miss Chris too, but that's another lost feeling of the heart. That's like a hole in my heart. I just want to cry. I'm so crabby. I want to kill Gina, elevate Bill, and befriend Chris H. Well whatever God gives me is right, so may my heart be open.

AT THIS TIME

Draw a Time-Life Map from the recent past up to the present moment. It could cover any period of time you want to review: a month, a week, etc.

Put the date of the beginning of this period on the left and today's date on the right. Then, above the line, write down the important events from this period in their chronological order.

Write a short story about one of the events on your list of recent events.

Looked for job—Sept. 4

Started job at L.C.'s—Sept. 6

Quit L.C.'s—Oct. 22

Started at Arby's—Nov. 4

Bought car—Nov. 10

Decided to customize car—Nov. 10

Started customizing—Jan. 21

Customizing Car: Well, I bought an '81 Chevy Malibu (station wagon). I'm going to get a new paint job, and redo the interior. Best of all I'm putting an outrageous SOUND SYSTEM in it. I'm going to take it to shows; I'll win trophies, because my car will be original (NOT GENERIC). By next summer I'll have a BAD ride. Nobody will touch it.

Sept. 4   Got pregnant

1st 3 months—morning sickness

2nd 3 months—getting fat

Beginning last 3 months—stretch marks

middle of this 3 months—baby kicking

last mo.—labor pains—doctors
contractions—baby is born

First months—baby gets bigger
rolls over
crawls
sits
stands
walks
teeth
first words

The first time Joshua moved inside me I was about five months pregnant. I was eating spaghetti and Italian sausage. Joshua kicked me so hard I fell off my chair. He moved from then on especially at night. I miss it now. It was the most weirdest feeling ever.

A DAY IN THE LIFE

Write about the worst thing that has happened to you in the recent past, such as the most embarrassing, most painful, scariest, saddest. How did you feel at the time? How do you feel about it now? What did you learn about yourself?

Write about the best day in your recent past. What happened? How did you feel then? How do you feel about it now? What did you learn?

When you are having difficulty in your life, what are some of the ways you can help yourself feel better? Make a list. (See example following.) As you discover new ways to feel better, add to your list. Be sure your choices are healthy for you; for instance, drugs or alcohol may make you think you feel better for a while but then you feel much worse after they've worn off.

WAYS TO HELP MYSELF FEEL BETTER
- Talk to my best friend.
- Draw or write in my journal.
- Take a walk or a ride in nature.
- Play my favorite sport.
- Listen to music I like or play an instrument.
- Take a hot bath.
- Talk to an adult I trust and like.
- Talk to God or my Higher Power.

WHAT'S ON MY MIND

Think of one word that expresses what is uppermost in your mind right now. Is it a person? A thing? A place? A feeling?

Write down the key word at the top of the journal page. Then make a list of words that come to mind in connection to the key word. Don't think about it before writing the list. Just let the words flow out from your mind onto the page. One word will lead to another in a chain reaction. This is "free association" writing.

Read over your list and write down your reactions. What did you find out about the theme expressed by the word? What did you find out about yourself?

Write a poem with your key word as the title. The poem need not rhyme, but it can if you wish. Let your poem express how you feel about the word. For inspiration and ideas, look at your list of words from the "free association" writing.

Sleep . . . drowsiness

If a person works all night, and goes to school, it doesn't leave much time for sleep. It makes a person tired with the lack of sleep. Daydreaming is a result of no sleep, just as yawning and drowsiness.

Upset . . . irritated

I'm *upset* because a friend of mine has a big problem and I feel troubled because I can't help her this time through her problem. I'm unhappy because she is only 16 and is 2 months pregnant. I feel *irritated* with her parents because they won't let me see her and I'm getting tired of trying.

CURRENT CHALLENGES

Draw a picture of a challenge or problem you are facing in your life right now. Give the picture a title.

Write a conversation with the challenge you drew in your picture.

If the challenge is a person, write an imaginary conversation with him or her. If it is a situation,such as.grades, school, or a particular quality in yourself, have a dialogue with it the way you would with a person. Write the dialogue out as if it's the script for a play.

Look at your picture of the current challenge in your life. Now draw a new picture showing how you would *like the situation to be*. Then write about what you drew in your picture.

As many times as you like, complete the sentence:
If I had my way....

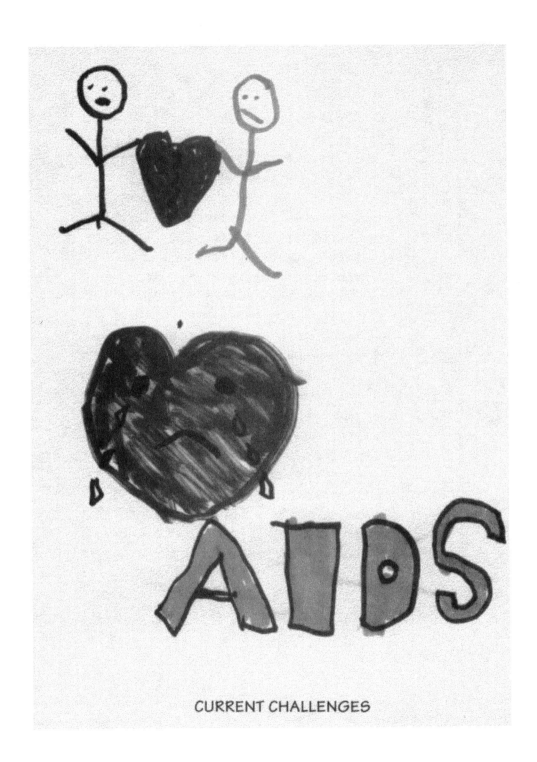

CURRENT CHALLENGES

Me: Hi, Scared, Confused. How are you?

Scared, Confused: I'm really confused and scared 'bout my "love" life. The guy I've "loved" for the past 4 1/2 yrs. really cares and my boyfriend now has cheated on me so many times and I take him back every time. Right now we are just friends. Which is OK Because now if things work out between me and D. . . .

Me: So what about AIDS?

Confused, Scared: Well I sleep with him along with other people. And never used protection. And D. and I talked and made me realize things I never realized before, and I'm really confused 'bout me and D. We hadn't talked in 2 mo. and now he's calling me.

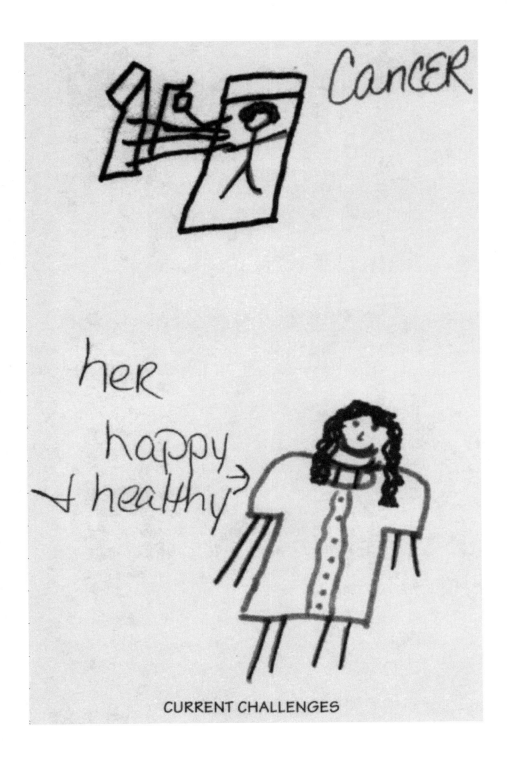

CURRENT CHALLENGES

If I had my way, she would be healthy. And happy. She wouldn't be lying in an ICU hospital bed. She'd be at home in her recliner watching "Jeopardy" like she usually does. If I had my way. But I don't.

Me: Why? Why her?

Cancer: Because.

Me: I don't want her to die. Not like this. Not now.

Cancer: Oh well.

Me: Why can't it be quick? Fast and painless? Why does she have to suffer? The treatment won't help or make it go away. She'll just suffer more and go through more agony. I don't understand.

CREATE YOUR OWN EXERCISE HERE

TITLE:

EXERCISE:

CREATE YOUR OWN EXERCISE HERE

TITLE:

EXERCISE:

CREATE YOUR OWN EXERCISE HERE

TITLE:

EXERCISE:

CREATE YOUR OWN EXERCISE HERE

TITLE:

EXERCISE:

CREATE YOUR OWN EXERCISE HERE

TITLE:

EXERCISE:

CHAPTER THREE

More About Me

The journey inward continues, the adventure that leads you back to yourself unfolds. This chapter has more activities for exploring who you are and where you're coming from. You'll be telling your own story, writing the script of your own life.

The events that have brought you to this place in your life are the stuff that movies and books are made of: everyday changes, big turning points, major passages from one period of life to another. We're all born, we all grow up, go to school, go out into the world. And through all of these trials and opportunities, we develop our view of the world, our personality, our skills and accomplishments. We face our own hurdles and find our own victories. Welcome to your inner world and the story of your life. It's a tale worth telling.

> *"I am young and possess many buried qualities; I am young and strong and am living a great adventure...Every day I feel that I am developing inward...."*

> **—Anne Frank, *Diary of a Young Girl***

SELF-PORTRAIT

Draw a picture of yourself. It can be a picture of how you look on the outside or how you feel inside. Or it can be both an inner portrait (feelings) and outer portrait (appearance).

_____

Look at your finished drawing and write down what you think it says about you.

_____

Imagine you are describing yourself to someone who has never seen you. Describe what you look like. Also write about your personality and anything else you think is important about you.

SELF-PORTRAIT

SELF-PORTRAIT

MY LIFE: HISTORY TIME LINE

Make a history time line similar to the one shown below. Put the year of your birth at the left side and the present year on the right side.

Above the line, write in the important events of your life. Use words, phrases, or sentences to describe each event. Place the events in the proper place on the time line and indicate the year or actual date if you remember it.

BORN in April 2 1975

——— Summer of 1989 I got my first Job

——— winter of 1990 I started Playing Hockey

——— Summer 1990 got my first car

MY LIFE

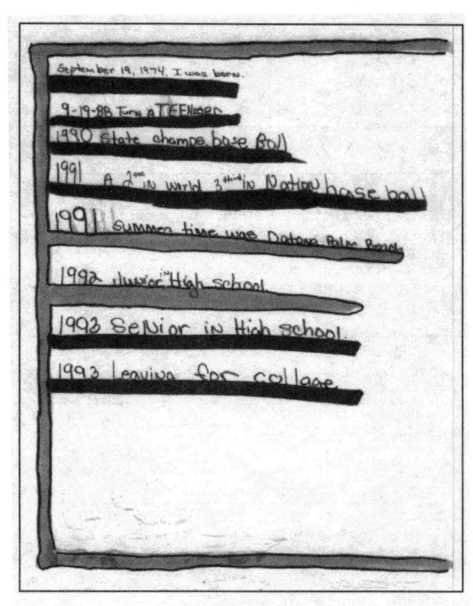

September 19, 1974. I was born.

9-19-88 Turn a TEENager

1990 State champs base Ball

1991 A 2ⁿᵈ in World 3ʳᵈ in Nation base ball

1991 summer time was Datona Palm Beach

1992 Junior in High school.

1992 Senior in High school.

1993 Leaving for collage.

MY LIFE

I REMEMBER

My First Memory

What is the very first thing you can remember? A place, a person, an object, an animal, or event? Draw a picture of it. Write about it.

When I Was Little

Write about a memory from your early years before you started school. Is it a memory of a person, place, a thing, an animal or pet, an event, a dream? Tell about how you felt at the time if you can recall the feelings. Then draw a picture of what you remember.

Starting School

Write about your first impressions when you started school. What do you remember? How did you feel? Describe people, places, events. Draw a picture of what you remember.

Growing Up

Pick something important from ages six through twelve and write about it as you did previously. Then draw a picture.

Growing Up Some More

Choose something that happened to you from age twelve to the present. Write about it and draw a picture.

MY STORY

Write your autobiography in five minutes. Include only the most important highlights.

Write a short biographical poem about yourself in the third person, as if you were writing about someone else. Don't worry about rhyming. Just let the words flow out.

Write a brief autobiography, starting with your birth and ending in the present. Use your history time line as an outline. Later, read over what you have written.

Select one event from your autobiography and draw a picture of it. Then write in detail about the scene you illustrated. Describe it in words: the setting, people, place, objects, and animals. What happened? How did you feel at the time? How do you feel about it now? What did you learn about yourself?

Illustrate other parts of your story if you wish, or choose particular events to write about in detail by describing the place, people, things, and the action.

GOING THROUGH CHANGES

Make a list of the important changes in your life, times when you started something new or ended something. Some examples are as follows:

- starting school.
- experiencing a new child in the family.
- having marriage in the family.
- dealing with separation or divorce.
- coping with illness or death.
- experiencing moving to a new neighborhood.
- changing schools or classes.
- travelling.
- dating.
- making a new friend.

Draw and write about one of the changes on your list. What happened? What was difficult at the time? How did you feel at the time? What did you learn from the experience? Have you become a better person as a result of what you went through? If so, how?

Pretend that you've met someone who is in the same kind of situation you described in the last piece. What would you tell that person to help him or her through the changes? Write it down.

Write about something humorous that happened as part of one of your changes.

Me: Hey, how's it going?

Self: Well, not too bad. But I'm a little nervous
        about after graduation, which path to go
        down. I know there is a right path and a
        wrong, but I'll choose the right, I hope.

Me: I'm sure you'll do fine.

WHO AM I?

Someone you have never met writes you a letter asking to be pen pals. Write back to this person. Introduce yourself, describe your appearance, your personality, your likes and dislikes. Include the things you like to do and the things you do well or know a lot about.

Look at yourself in the mirror and draw a portrait of yourself.

Write a poem in which you begin each line with the words, "I am.." Complete the sentence as many times as you wish. The poem doesn't have to rhyme, but it can if you wish.

"I have an odd way of sometimes being able to see myself through someone else's eyes. Then I view the affairs of a certain 'Anne' at my ease, browse through the pages of her life as if she were a stranger."

—**Anne Frank,** ***Diary of a Young Girl***

INSIDE/OUTSIDE

Draw a picture of how you think others see you on the outside. Use any style you like: doodles, cartoons, representational drawing.

Draw a picture of how you see yourself on the inside. Include feelings and thoughts, wishes and dreams.

Write about the two pictures. What did you discover about yourself? How do the pictures differ? In what ways are they alike?

How would you like others to see you? Write about it. Draw a picture.

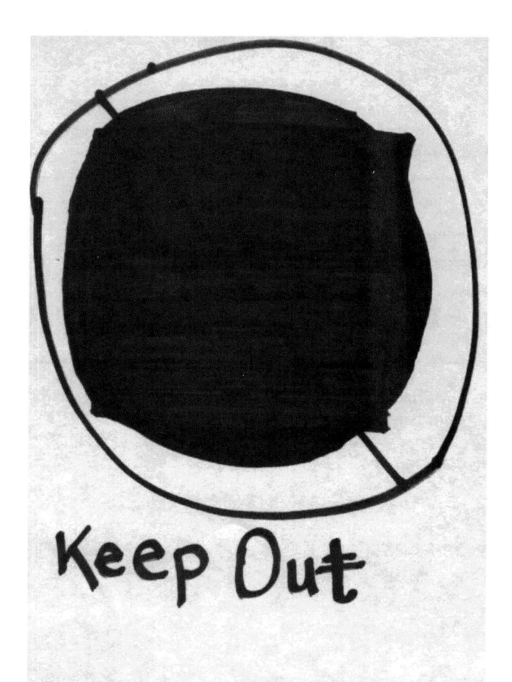

Others see me as some sad/troubled teenager who is in her own little world, and wants nobody to enter her little world, because they will always leave her blue (sad).

OTHeRS see me as happy.

AWARDS

You've just received an award for some achievement. Give the award a name and draw a picture of it. Write a proclamation of your award. It could be a letter from someone you admire. Tell when the award was given, where, by whom, and what it was for.

Smiles are free so don't save them.

This aware represents that I have a great sense of humor. I would say that this is my best quality. If you save up all those smiles and you die, nobody will know how you really are, and you will die unhappy.

 # 1 MUSIC LOVER OF THE YEAR

I received this award from myself, because I am not closed-minded like most people. I like all different kinds of music (from heavy metal to Bach). Most people don't admit they like a certain kind of music. If they would just listen to it, and not criticize it. I love music of all kinds. The award is for open-mindedness.

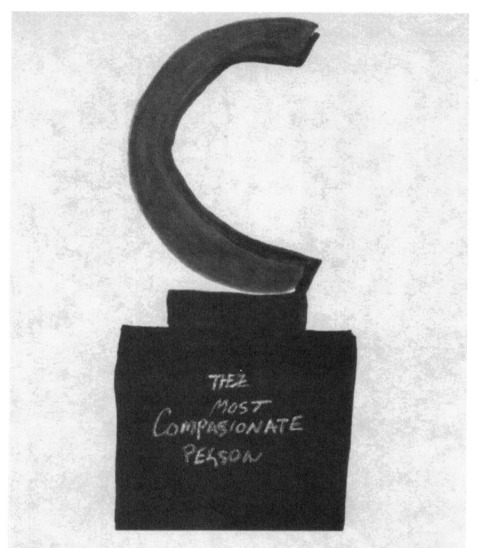

This award is for being the most compassionate, for feeling deep sympathy and sorrow for another's suffering or misfortune, and also a desire to ease their pain or remove the cause of the action. So we give this compassion award of the year
to
Michael R.
He is one of the few who cares about his family's and friends' suffering and to help them get through it at all times. So congratulations to you and keep up the good work.

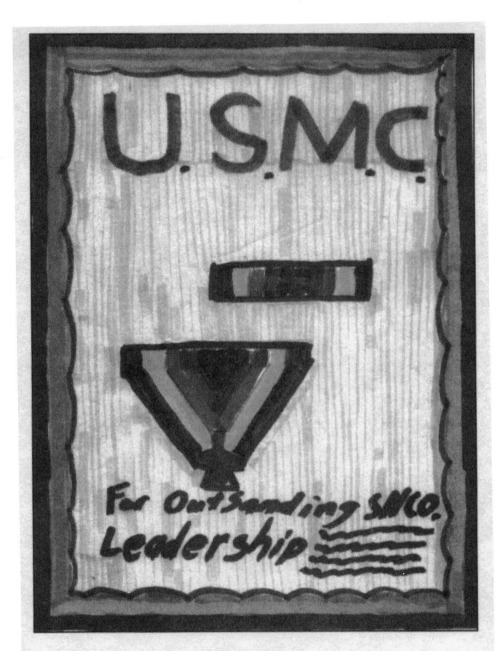

I received the staff-NCO leadership award for outstanding SNCO excellence and leadership qualities. U.S.M.C.

CREATE YOUR OWN EXERCISE HERE

TITLE:

EXERCISE:

CREATE YOUR OWN EXERCISE HERE

TITLE:

EXERCISE:

CREATE YOUR OWN EXERCISE HERE

TITLE:

EXERCISE:

CREATE YOUR OWN EXERCISE HERE

TITLE:

EXERCISE:

CHAPTER FOUR

Getting It All Together

We all enter the world into a family, a culture, a place on the planet. We learn customs, rules, and regulations at home, in school, and in our community. The adults who take care of us in childhood—parents, guardians, teachers—have their own attitudes and beliefs. We learn these as we are growing up.

In the teen years (as you prepare for your own adult life) you begin asking questions. You start forming beliefs, ideas, and values based on your own experiences. You are preparing to create your own adult life. This is normal and natural. But often teenagers are made to feel wrong or guilty for questioning the way things are. You want to find your own way, form your own thoughts and opinions, and shape your own life, but adults may be afraid of your need to become your own person.

Sometimes teenagers think that rebelling against adults is the only way to create a life of their own. That is not necessarily true. The important thing is to think and to reflect upon yourself and what kind of life you want rather than reacting against what others want and believe. This chapter will help you to do just that.

THIS IS YOUR LIFE

You have been hired to write a TV series based on your life. Give it a title. Create fictitious names, if you like. Who are the leading characters? Describe each one of them. How are they related or connected to each other? Where do they live? Go to school? Work? Hang out? What do they like to do? What challenges do they face?

_____

Write a description of one "episode" of the TV series based on your life. Base it on a true event or situation. Who are the main characters in this particular story? What problems or challenges do they face? What happens? How do the characters change (learn something, become stronger, more tolerant, more creative, etc.)?

_____

Describe another episode of your TV series. This time create a situation or event that you would like to have happen in real life. Perhaps it's a recurring wish or daydream. Who are the main characters? What happens? How do the people in the story change? How do you change?

GETTING IT ALL TOGETHER

We have different parts to our personalities. We all have qualities or abilities such as creativity, courage, intelligence, a sense of humor, friendliness, talent, etc. Think about your qualities and make a list of them.

Draw a jigsaw puzzle with one of your qualities written onto each puzzle piece. You may also want to draw designs or use colors that express each quality.

Write a short poem about each quality. Use the name of the quality as the poem's title.

Generous

To be generous is to be kind.
To be kind is to be courteous.
To be courteous is to be consistent.
To be consistent is to be respectful.
To be respectful is to be loving.
To be loving is to be noble.
To be noble is to be responsible.
To be responsible is to have will power.

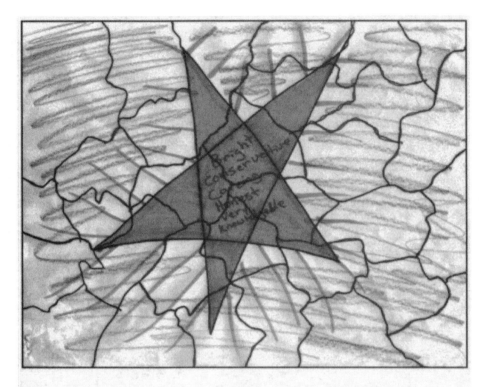

Caring

Caring is the word to describe myself.
Caring is another word for respect.
When you have respect it means you care.
When you care it makes a difference in the world.

faithful
courageous
creative
compassionate
noble
respectful
helpful
honest
friendly
nice

Faithful

Men and women look around
Some people smile the others frown
The men look at women as they walk by
Some women stop when the men say Hi
The women stay and think they're cool
I look away because I'm FAITHFUL

WHO I AM BECOMING

Who we are is an expression of our personality traits. Think of a personality trait that you would like to have, such as generosity, sensitivity to the needs of others, honesty, courage, diligence, discipline, responsibility, kindness, creativity. At the top of a new page write down the desired quality, then write a poem or a paragraph about that quality. You may also want to draw a picture of yourself expressing that personality trait in your life.

Write out a plan on how to develop this quality in yourself. Be specific. What actions can you take each day? How will you chart your progress in your journal?

Think of a skill that you would like to learn or develop, such as driving a car, drawing, playing tennis, playing a musical instrument, singing, using a computer, or carpentry. Name the skill you want to learn and describe it. Picture yourself having mastered this skill. Then draw a picture of yourself using that skill. Describe what it's like to have reached your goal. Then write about what you will need to develop this skill: a coach, written or verbal instructions, materials or equipment, hands-on experience, practice. Make a plan. Be specific.

MY BODY/MYSELF

Draw an outline of your body. If there are any parts of your body that hurt or are a "problem," color those areas on your body chart. Use colors that express how you feel in those parts of your body.

Pretend that each area of your body can talk. Interview each body part you colored in on your chart. Ask the following questions and write down the answers:

      1. Who are you? (What specific body part are you?)
      2. How do you feel?
      3. Why do you feel this way?
      4. What can I do to help you?

MY PHILOSOPHY OF LIFE

Write down your philosophy of life. What things are most important to you? What do you need in order to be happy?

What kinds of people and human qualities do you admire most? Do you know anyone who is "living" according to your philosophy of life? Name the person or people and describe how they are living examples of your philosophy of life. If they have written or said anything that reveals their philosophy, write it down in your journal as inspiration.

"I can recapture everything when I write... Anyone who doesn't write doesn't know how wonderful it is; I used to bemoan the fact that I couldn't draw at all, but now I am more than happy that I can at least write. And if I haven't any talent for writing books or newspaper articles, well then I can always write for myself."

—Anne Frank, *Diary of a Young Girl*

I BELIEVE

Make a list of all the things you believe about yourself.

───────────────────────────────

Circle the beliefs that are negative.

───────────────────────────────

On another page, rewrite each negative belief as a positive one, as shown following. Write your new belief in the present tense as if it were already a reality. Use your imagination to create the best positive statements you can.

Old belief: "I'm a poor student."

New belief: "I have help and am studying and learning more every day."

Old belief: "I hate writing. My writing is terrible and I'll never be able to write properly."

New belief: "The more I write in my journal, the better my writing gets. I really enjoy writing now."

LIKES AND DISLIKES

Write a list of things you like to do. Then make a list of things you don't like to do.

Describe one of the things from each list and why you like or don't like to do it.

Write a poem about the things you like (people, things, activities, food, colors, etc.). You can title the poem, "I Like... ," and repeat that opening line throughout. Your poem can rhyme if you want it to, but that's not necessary.

Illustrate your poem.

Dislike:
    I do not want to be in this boring town.

Like:
    I would like to graduate, travel, see places,
    and faces.

Surfing is happiness
Surfing is love
Peace is excitement
Peace is a dove

I like to fly planes. It first came into my life when I was just fifteen years old. It relaxes me and the world looks so small and everyone looks like ants.

WHAT I'M GOOD AT

Think of something you do well. Imagine you are watching a movie of yourself. Picture yourself doing the activity you do well. See it one step at a time.

When we are good at doing something, it's important to share our knowledge and skills with others. Write out instructions telling someone how to do the thing you do well. Make it clear and simple and, if it would help, include pictures or diagrams. You can number the steps in the procedure if you wish. Be sure to include a list of materials if your activity requires them. Your instructions should be so clear that someone could do the activity after reading what you've written.

HOBBIES AND PASTIMES

What are your hobbies? Write about one of them. Describe what you do in this hobby. Why do you like to do it? How do you feel when you're doing it? What have you learned or accomplished by having this hobby?

If you don't have any hobbies, write down some that you think you'd like. Give your reasons for being interested in these particular hobbies.

Choose a hobby you'd like to pursue and write down how you can get started. What will you need—information, a teacher, time, materials or equipment, a place? Make a plan.

What are your favorite pastimes? What activities in your life give you the most pleasure and satisfaction? Describe your favorite pastime and the feelings you get from it.

THE NEW ME

Draw a picture of yourself the way you'd like to be.

Write a description of the "new you" (yourself as you'd like to be). Include physical appearance, personality, qualities, achievements, experiences. Give all the details. Write down how you'd feel if you were the person you just drew.

ANSWERING BACK:
"DOWN WITH PUT-DOWNS"

When we're growing up, we all get negative criticism or ridicule from others at one time or another. It makes us feel "put down" and less than our true selves. It's easy to believe those put-downs, remember them, and carry them around in our heads. It's like a tape recording playing in our brains. We keep playing back the tape over and over and then it becomes the voice of our own Inner Critic. The Inner Critic quietly nags at us and eats away at our self-esteem.

This exercise helps you to identify the Inner Critic so that you can choose whether to let it nag you or not. It also lets you have your real feelings about being talked to that way. We feel hurt and angry when we are put down but may not be able to express it. Here's a chance to let those feelings out.

On the left side of the page, write down all the critical things you think or say about yourself. Write it as if someone were saying it to you, such as, "You'll never be popular with other kids. Who would want you for a friend?" This is your Inner Critic speaking. This may take more than one page. Remember to leave the right side of the page blank.

Now read all the put-downs your Inner Critic wrote. Then let yourself feel your reactions. It's OK to let yourself get angry. Then, on the right side of the page you get to "answer back" to each of those criticisms. Put the pen in your other hand. Yes, that's right. Switch hands and use the one you don't normally write with. The writing or printing with the other hand may feel and look awkward. But try it anyway. You may feel like a little child. That's fine because there is a child inside all of us who has feelings that need to be recognized. Writing or printing with the other (nondominant) hand can help us bring out these childlike feelings within.

With your nondominant hand, answer back to each put down. Say whatever you feel. Don't worry about penmanship, spelling, or grammar. Just let your feelings out.

One student who thought he couldn't write with his nondominant hand did the following dialogue using only his nondominant hand:

> Me: I CAN'T WRITE WITH MY LEFT HAND.
> Hand: YES YOU CAN.
> Me: NO I CAN'T.
> Hand: WELL YOU JUST DID.
> Me: OH I GUESS I DID, DIDN'T I?
> Hand: YOU SURE DID.
> Me: THANK YOU.
> Hand: YOU'RE WELCOME.

The same student did this drawing of his left hand holding the pen.

Dominant Hand

Nondominant Hand

You're so stupid! You'll never get good grades in school, so give up on that. And no one really likes you. Your so-called friends just feel sorry for you. You couldn't even get a date for the prom so that dad to fix you up with someone.

Let's face it, you're a mess. Your face is broken out. You are too fat and you don't know how to dress. You pathetic loser!

OH SHUT UP! I'M SICK + TIRED OF YOUR LIES. THE BIGGEST PROBLEM IN MY LIFE IS YOU + YOUR PUT DOWNS. SHUT UP BECAUSE I'M NOT LISTENING TO YOU ANYMORE!

This dialogue, done by a teenage girl, allowed her to answer back to her Inner Critic and stand up for herself.

TAKING CARE OF MYSELF

Make a list of all the ways in which you treat yourself well,such as, do things you like to do, spend time with people who treat you with love and respect, go places where you feel peaceful and happy, achieve goals you've set for yourself, appreciate yourself. Label the list "Treats."

Write a list of things that upset you in some way: illness, fear, hurt, etc. Label the list "Upsets." Then take each of the upsets and write down what good things you can do to help yourself feel calm, safe, peaceful, healthy, etc. when you experience that particular upset. Turn upsets into treats.

Write a love letter to yourself describing all the things you like about yourself. Write it as if you were addressing someone very special in your life. Begin it with Dear Self.

Write a poem entitled "I Need," in which you talk about all the things you need in order to feel physically healthy, good about yourself, happy, and content.

I need . . .
Love above all . . .
   to love myself and be
      a good friend to myself.

I need . . .
to be touched by something
   outside myself
      both physically and spiritually.
I need . . .
to move my body
   to dance
      or do Tai Chi
         or move my body in some way.
I need . . .
to let my creativity out . . .
   to let myself out . . .
      to have an exchange
         with what is around me,
            input and output.
I need air
   and nature
      and to understand and experience
         the origins of the world . . .
            the forests, the life . . .
I need freedom
   to live my life
      as I see fit
         to go outside for walks
            at night if I want . . .
               to run my own existence
I need . . .
   to be me and be allowed to be me.

CREATE YOUR OWN EXERCISE HERE

TITLE:

EXERCISE:

CREATE YOUR OWN EXERCISE HERE

TITLE:

EXERCISE:

CREATE YOUR OWN EXERCISE HERE

TITLE:

EXERCISE:

ME AND OTHERS

CHAPTER FIVE

Me and Others

The journal is a good place to reflect upon how you feel about others. Sometimes you have feelings about others that you're afraid to express: anger, resentment, fear, jealousy. You might not express these feelings for fear of hurting the other person. Or perhaps you're afraid he or she might react and hurt or punish you. In your journal, you can let your emotions out honestly without having to deal with the reactions of others. In this way, you can accept all your feelings instead of letting them build up inside you.

You can also explore your loving feelings toward others and learn to put these feelings into words. By developing an "attitude of gratitude" you can build stronger bridges between yourself and others, creating a safer and more supportive atmosphere. Peace and love on our planet start with each one of us taking responsibility for how we relate to others.

"In spite of everything I still believe that people are really good at heart."

—Anne Frank, ***Diary of a Young Girl***

FAMILY PORTRAIT

Draw a picture of yourself with your family. This can be the family you live with or your extended family, including step-parents, grandparents, aunts, uncles, cousins. Include pets or others who you consider to be a part of your family.

_____

Have each family member tell his or her name. This can be done in "balloons" (like the ones used in comic strips), on t-shirts, hats, or any other part of the picture.

_____

Have each family member "speak" in the first person and say something about him or herself. Write down what each one says.

_____

Write down how you feel about each family member in your picture.

FAMILY TREE

Make a family tree diagram. Fill in the names of each of your family members. If you have more than one family grouping because of divorce, death, or remarriage, make a family tree for each family.

Write something about each person in your family tree. Include such things as qualities, talents, achievements. Also include things you've learned from each person.

PARENTS

Write a letter to your parents or guardians or any other adults who are in a parental role in your life. This letter is just for you, so don't send it. Tell them how you feel about them, what you receive from them, what you give them. If there is anything you would like to change between you, say so in your letter.

Repeat the activity above, but this time write the letter to your grandparents or members of your family with whom you are in close contact. Remember, this letter is just for you. However, if you decide to write a letter to be sent you may want to use this one as the raw material for the one you share.

MY FAVORITE PERSON

Who is your favorite person in all the world? Draw a picture of this person. It can be someone living or dead.

Write a letter telling why you like this person so much. What do you admire about this person? Has this person achieved something in life that you would like to achieve? If so, what is it? What have you received from this person? What have you learned? Express your gratitude in this letter. This letter is meant for your journal, but you might want to send a copy of it to the person later on.

Make a list of all the personality traits and qualities you admire in your favorite person. Imagine that you have been given these qualities as a gift. How would your life be different now that you have these traits? Give a specific example of how you'd be or do things differently. For instance, if patience is one of the qualities, you might use it in dealing with a particular person or situation that is frustrating for you.

MY SUPPORT SYSTEM

Draw a picture or diagram showing yourself and the people who support you and help you and who you support and help in some way. Show how you relate to the others in your support system.

Write about each person. How do they support and help you? How do you support and help them?

Describe your relationship to all of these people in detail. Write about what you give and do not give to each other, what you're satisfied with and what you're dissatisfied with about the relationship.

Write a "thank you" note to each of these people. Express your gratitude for all the ways each person helps you. Write the notes in your journal but, if it feels right to you, do a "thank you" note that you actually send. You decide which people you want to send notes to.

MY SUPPORT SYSTEM

LETTER TO SOMEONE

Think of someone you have a problem with in your life at this time. With no intention to send it, write a letter to this person in your journal. In this letter tell the person how you feel about him or her. Be completely honest and tell the person exactly what's on your mind: all the things you've wanted to say, but haven't. Include in the letter why you haven't been able to tell the person these things directly.

In the second part of your letter, tell the person how you would like things to be between you.

Now, pretend that this person is there with you. Write down his or her reaction to what you just shared. If it feels right, you may want to respond and continue a written conversation between the two of you in which both points of view are expressed.

IF I WERE A PARENT

Imagine that you are a parent. What kind of relationship would you want to have with your child? How would you raise your child? What kind of rules and limits would you set? What kinds of rewards would you give? Write about it.

Think about some major conflicts you've had with your own parents or guardians. Picture yourself as a parent and realistically describe how you would deal with these problems with your own child. Write it as a dialogue with your imaginary child. You become the parent; the other person is your child. Write it out as the script for a play. (See example following.)

Parent: You stayed out too late again.

Teenager: No I didn't. All the other kids were out as late as I was.

Parent: This is between you and me, not the other kids or their parents. You were out way after nine o'clock.

Teenager: Yeah, but you never told me exactly what time to come home. You just said don't stay out too late. How late is too late?

Parent: You're right. We never agreed on a time. I'd like you in by 9:00 P.M.

Teenager: Even on weekends?

Parent: OK ten on Fridays and Saturdays.

IF I WERE A TEACHER

Imagine that you are a schoolteacher. Write down your ideas and theories about education. How do you think teachers should relate to students? How should students relate to teachers? How would you handle some of the following: classroom discipline, homework, motivating students to learn? Write about it.

Think of a few typical problems that you have seen at school: absenteeism, tardiness, unruly behavior, drugs, theft, fighting. Make a list of your own school problems based on your observations. How would you handle these problems if you were a teacher?

If you were a teacher how would you keep your students interested in learning? How would you present information and what activities would you assign? Be creative and innovative. Write about it. How would you encourage and reward students? How would you discipline them if they were behaving destructively or disrespectfully toward others?

A REAL PAL

Do you have a best friend? When and where did you meet? Write about it. Include comments about your first impression of this person who became your best friend.

Draw a picture of your best friend. Then write a detailed description of your best friend: physical appearance, personality, mannerisms, habits, likes and dislikes, talents and achievements.

Describe differences and similarities between you and your best friend. What do you have in common? What interests do you share? What things do you disagree or argue about?

Write about why you are friends with this person. Would you like to change your friendship in any way? If so, how would you like it to be?

What do you think friends should do for each other? How do you want your friends to treat you? How do you treat your friends?

Write about a time when you helped your friend in a difficult situation. What happened and how did you help?

Helping a Friend

A long time ago just right before I came to this country, the USA, in my country I had a good friend. One day it happened that he came for my advice. And he told me what was wrong.* And he asked me, "What do you think?" I told him, "Before you do anything or before I tell you what to do, I think you and I should go to see if what you told me is right or not." So we went and he WAS right.

So I advised him not to do anything that he would regret. A few days before this, I had asked him if I could do something for him. Anyway I counseled him, "Wait for a few days before you do something. Don't do anything while you're upset." After a few days, the problem that he had solved itself and he thanked me for getting him to wait for that few days.

*Sorry, I'm not telling what the problem was because I promised him I would not tell anybody.

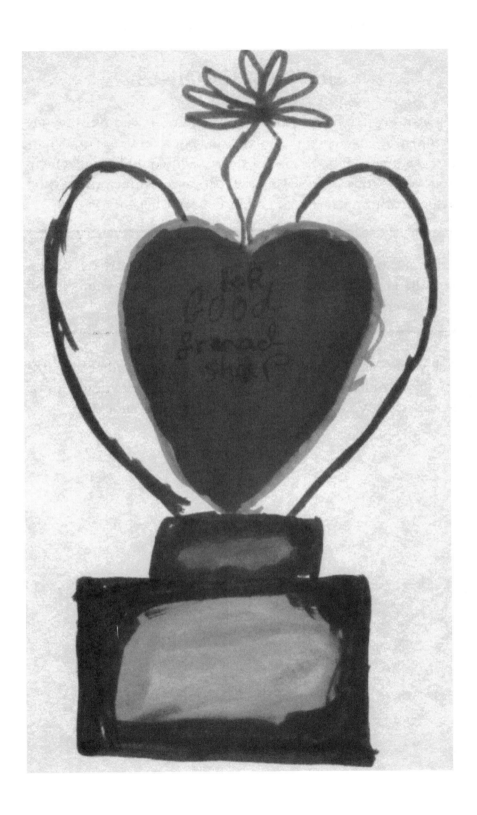

HEROES/HEROINES

Choose a well-known person you admire. It can be someone living, dead, or fictional. It may be a historical figure or a character in a movie, book, or TV show. Or it could be someone in your community. Describe the person's characteristics and achievements and why you admire him or her.

Imagine yourself meeting this person. Describe the occasion and the environment. Write a conversation with your "hero" or "heroine."

Ask your "hero" or "heroine" to give you some advice regarding any problem you are facing in your life. Write down his or her answer. What would he or she do in your shoes?

TOP TEN

Write a list of people you like the most. Choose people you know or have known. These people can be living or dead as long as you have known them personally.

———————————————————

Next to each person's name, write down their qualities or achievements which you like most.

———————————————————

Taking each person one at a time, write down in what ways you would want to be like each one of them.

———————————————————

Choose your favorite person from the list you made. Draw a picture of the two of you doing something together.

———————————————————

Imagine that you are meeting with this person one-to-one. Write out a conversation between the two of you. Are there any questions you want to ask, anything you want to know? What do you want this person to know about you? Tell what you like about him or her.

DON'T LIKE

Make a list of people's actions that you don't like. What particular behaviors really bother you?

_____

Make a list of people you don't like. Write down what you dislike about each person. Is it personality traits, behavior, attitudes? Then write down anything you like or envy about each one of these people.

_____

If you could give each one of these people a "magic gift" that would help improve him or her, what would it be? Complete the following sentence for each person on your list:

I would like to give _____ the gift of _____ .
                        (person)   (desired quality)

_____

Picture each person on your list one at a time. Imagine how they'd look and act if they had the qualities you wished for them.

FIGHTING

Fake
Wrong
Right
Stupid
Selfish
Conceited
Insecure
Outcast
Tough
Wimp
Difference
Scary
Sad
Mean

Who gives us the right?
Why do we have to fight?
It's so very dumb
    and so selfish and mean,
It just makes me scream.
I can't even watch,
It's so confusing.
The reasons are so many,
    and there are so many different
    people
    with different values.
There's no real explanation
    for any of it

INVENT-A-FRIEND

Using your imagination, create an ideal friend. Write a letter to your imaginary friend telling him or her your feelings and experiences.

"Dear Kitty,
The sun is shining, the sky is deep blue, there is a lovely breeze and I'm longing—so longing—for everything. To talk, for freedom, for friends, to be alone. And I do so long...to cry! I feel as if I'm going to burst, and I know that it would get better with crying; but I can't, I'm restless, I go from one room to the other, breathe through the crack of a closed window, feel my heart beating, as if it is saying, 'Can't you satisfy my longings at last?'

I believe that it is spring within me, I feel that spring is awakening, I feel it in my whole body and soul. It is an effort to behave normally, I feel utterly confused, don't know what to read, what to write, what to do, I only know that I am longing...!
Yours, Anne"

—Anne Frank, *Diary of a Young Girl*

MY IDEAL PARTNER

If you could create a partner or a mate, what kind of person would it be? Describe the person's appearance, personality, likes and dislikes, activities, work, hobbies. What does your ideal partner value? What's most important to him or her? Write about it.

___

List all the ways you and your ideal partner are similar and all the ways you are different.

___

How would you and your ideal partner interact with each other? What kinds of things would you do together? How would you treat each other? How would you feel about yourself when you were with this person? How do you think he or she would feel being with you?

CREATE YOUR OWN EXERCISE HERE

TITLE:

EXERCISE:

CREATE YOUR OWN EXERCISE HERE

TITLE:

EXERCISE:

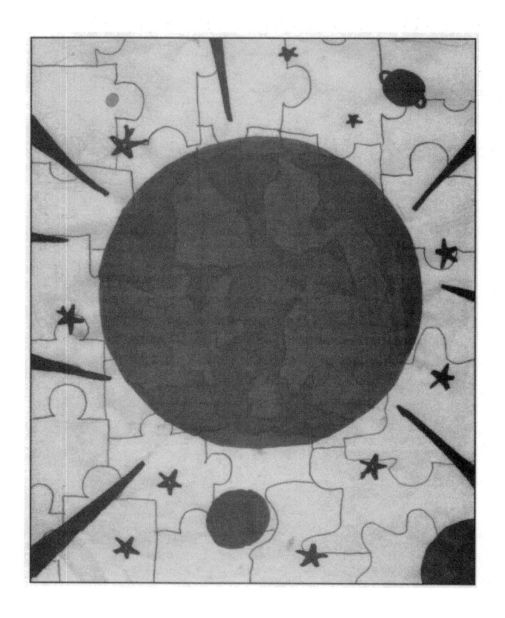

CHAPTER SIX

My World

Common experiences of daily life have always inspired writers and artists. The world you live in, the things that surround you, are wonderful subjects for drawing and writing. As you record your sense impressions of these simple everyday places and things, you develop skills in observation, communication, but also appreciation.

> *"The best remedy for those who are afraid, lonely, or unhappy is to go outside, somewhere where they can be quiet alone with the heavens, nature, and God. Because only then does one feel that all is as it should be and that God wishes to see people happy, amidst the simple beauty of nature. As long as this exists, and it certainly always will, I know then that there will always be comfort for every sorrow, whatever the circumstance may be. And I firmly believe that nature brings solace in all troubles."*

> —**Anne Frank,** *Diary of a Young Girl*

BACK TO NATURE

Imagine that you are out in nature. Where are you and what do you see around you? Draw a picture of the scene.

Write a dialogue with some aspect of the scene you drew. Some suggestions are:

- a flower.
- a plant or tree.
- the weather.
- an animal.

Now choose an animate or inanimate object in your scene. Write a paragraph or a poem as if you were that thing.

Describe a beautiful experience you have had in nature. Where were you? Write down all the impressions you took in with your senses: seeing, hearing, smelling. How did you feel at the time?

Me: Hi! Weather. How are you today?

Weather: I feel beautiful today.

Me: Why is that?

Weather: Because the wind is blowing and the cool breeze is blazing across the clear blue sky and the sound of the ocean wind.

Me: Weather, the wind is running through my hair as I run through the mountain. I feel the breeze rising against me. The rain in the forest sounds wonderful. The flowers smell just beautiful.

MY FAVORITE THINGS

Choose your favorite thing. It may be a favorite article of clothing, your car, a piece of jewelry. Draw a picture of your favorite thing.

Write about the favorite thing in your drawing. Describe what it looks and feels like. Tell how it came into your life. Why is it your favorite thing? How do you use it? If you lost it or if it were taken away from you, how would you feel and what would you do?

The object I picked is my flute. It's silver and has a lot of keys. Things reflect off of it. I started playing flute when I was in seventh grade. My friend D. and I decided to go out for band and chorus to get rid of frustrations. That was in Vermont. Now the only time I play it usually is when I'm depressed or bored and usually it cheers me up and sometimes other people. I would be really upset and break things if it were taken away.

My favorite thing that I own is my car. I got it myself about two months ago. If it were taken away I would be upset. The only thing I use it for is mostly to go to school and work, and when I have time I go to a friend's house or shop and to the race track.

My favorite objects are pictures. Pictures of memories or pretty places. This one I drew is of a pretty picture I love, grass and tree scenery. They are just so pretty. I like this kind of scenery because it brings peace into my life. Well, if I lost it or it was taken away from me I'd either be dead or blind. I don't know what I'd do without colors.

My favorite object is my stereo because I listen to music a lot. Like, to put me to sleep, wake me up, or when I'm just there. I got it for Christmas two years ago and if I lost it I guess I would save money to buy another one.

Teddy bear is one of the things I like most. I call it Rainbow because it has different colors on it. Rainbow is fifteen inches tall. My mom got Rainbow for me last Christmas. I use it as my pillow and I like to take Rainbow everywhere I go. If Rainbow was taken away from me I'd be very sad. What I'd do is to go to the store and find one exactly like Rainbow.

MY SPACE

Draw a picture of your room or space at home. Describe the room (or part of the room) that is yours.

Write about how your room or area expresses your personality. What do you like about your room or area? What don't you like about it?

If you could make your room or area exactly as you wished, how would that look? Draw a picture of the way you'd like it to be. Write a description of it as well.

MY HOME

Write about the place where you live. Describe it: the outside and inside. What do you like about living there? What don't you like about living there?

If you could, what would you change about the place you live? How would your life be different if these changes were made?

How is your room or area similar to the rest of the house? How is it different?

MY SCHOOL

Divide your paper into two halves with headings Pro and Con. In the Pro column, write a list of reasons a person should attend your school.

In the Con column, write another list describing why a student should not attend your school.

PRO	CON

THE IDEAL SCHOOL

Imagine that you have been asked to design the ideal school from the ground up. You can have any type of buildings in any location. Draw a picture of your ideal school. Include a floor plan to show all the areas.

In your ideal school, you can create the rules and policies. You are also in charge of the educational program as well as all other school activities. Describe your rules and regulations. Write about your educational program. Describe other school activities that you would include.

Describe what kinds of teachers and staff members you would hire. What kind of students would attend your ideal school?

MY FAVORITE PLACE

Imagine that you are in a very special place you've been before. You truly enjoyed yourself there. Return there in your imagination, move around, and look at everything that surrounds you. This may be someone's house, a church, restaurant, amusement park, or place in nature. Draw a picture of yourself in this special place.

Write about the special place. Where was it? How do you feel about the place? What did you do when you went there in your imagination?

WHAT I WEAR

Draw a picture of yourself in the clothes you usually wear every day. Write about how your clothes express your personality.

Draw yourself in your favorite clothes or outfit. How do you feel when you wear these clothes?

Design and draw an outfit of clothing you would like to have.

FOOD

Make a list of your favorite foods. Describe a favorite eating experience. Where were you? What did you eat? What did the food look like, taste like, smell like? Here's one student's list:

Lasagna
Spaghetti
Pizza
Tacos
Salads
Steak
Potatoes
Vegetables
Fruit
Chicken
Roast beef
Cakes and cookies
Ham
Eggs and bacon

Describe the perfect meal. Use your imagination to create the menu, place, atmosphere. Describe the experience in detail.

Write out a recipe for something you know how to cook. List the ingredients first, then list the procedures in numbered order, as in a cookbook.

I usually eat at home. My grandfather is a good cook. I like
the way he cooks seafood. It looks like it has everything, like
vegetables, color, and seafood. The taste is so good and it's
my family's favorite. The smell is so sweet and makes you
hungry.

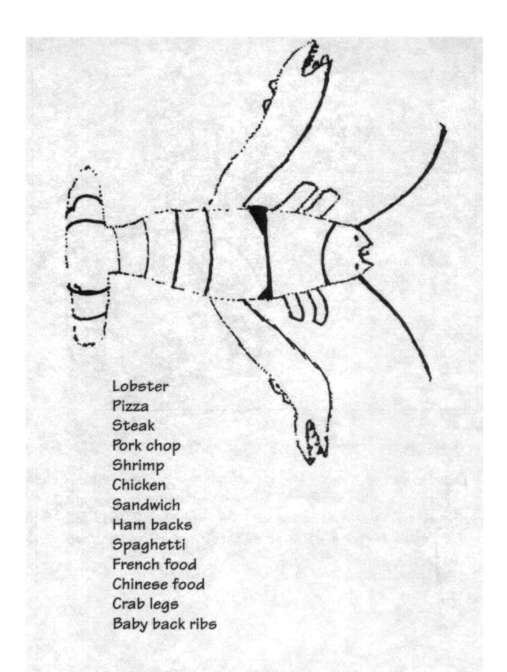

Lobster
Pizza
Steak
Pork chop
Shrimp
Chicken
Sandwich
Ham backs
Spaghetti
French food
Chinese food
Crab legs
Baby back ribs

I went to Red Lobster for dinner. I ordered lobster and French fries, bread too. The hot lobster was steaming and the butter too. I broke off the claw and opened it up and dipped it into the butter. It tasted really good.

Tofu sandwich
Beans and rice
Bean taco
Veggies and cheese sub sandwich

I sat in a room listening to music and eating beans and rice. Then went to sleep after I drank a glass of water. The mus was SKINNY PUPPIES tape ANTI-VIVISECTION V. It was oud but didn't cause a headache. It was at night. The foowas warm and was seasoned.

FRUIT SALAD

How to Make a Fruit Salad

What you need:

Lettuce (3-4 leaves)	Watermelon (1/2)
Apples (2)	Bowl
Grapes (bunch)	Knife
Lemon (1)	Cutting board
Oranges (2)	Lemon juice
Banana (1)	Orange juice
Cherries (fresh bunch)	Cottage cheese

1. Take your bowl and put lettuce leaves at the bottom so they cover the sides or stick up.
2. Cut the apple in 1/4 slices, lemon in 1/4 slices, oranges in 1/4 slices (peel the skin), cut banana into slices and watermelon into bits.
3. Put some of cottage cheese in bottom of bowl about 1/4 the way up.
4. Put in some (not all) of the grapes, cherries and watermelon bits.
5. Put the rest of the cottage cheese over the fruit.
6. Put the apple slices around the edge sticking up between the oranges and lemons.
7. Put the banana slices after those like so.
8. Now, in the middle put the rest of the cherries, grapes, and watermelon.
9. Take the lemon juice and orange juice, mix them together (having more lemon juice). Pour it over the fruit lightly.

Arabic Meat loaf

A leaf of parsley   1 teaspoon spices mixed together
3 onions   1 teaspoon of salt
3 pounds of chopped meat   1 bag brown gravy mix

Chop the parsley to really small pieces and also the onion.

Mix the parsley with the onion then put all the spices and salt on the chopped onion and parsley.

Then mix the meat well. Then put the mix of onion and parsley onto the meat and mix well.

Put it in a pan and put it in the oven for 45 minutes.

While the meat is cooking, you cook the gravy.

The Taco

Makes 4 tacos

Ingredients:

1/2 cup lettuce (optional)
1 cup cheese
4 large or small taco shells
1 pkg. taco seasoning

12 tablespoons hot sauce
(optional)
Hamburger meat
(as much as you wish)

First you brown the hamburger. Then add the seasoning. Then stir and put the meat on one of the shells (as much or as little as you wish). Then make it to suit you with the ingredients listed above. Or you can use any ingredients you so desire.

CREATE YOUR OWN EXERCISE HERE

TITLE:

EXERCISE:

CREATE YOUR OWN EXERCISE HERE

TITLE:

EXERCISE:

CHAPTER SEVEN

Creating My Future

Many people go through life thinking they are the victims of circumstance, that they have no control over their lives. It is true that we cannot control what others think, say, or do. And there are many other situations over which we have no control, such as death and natural disasters. But we do have control over how we think, and what we say and do. That's what this chapter is about.

An artist is inspired to paint a picture, gets the paint and canvas, and then puts the idea into material form. You can do the same with your life. You have control over your own vision of the kind of future you want. With your imagination, something that all humans have but not everyone uses constructively, you have the power to create your own life. Go for it!

"I want to go on living even after my death! And therefore I am grateful to God for giving me this gift, this possibility of developing myself and of writing, of expressing all that is in me."

—Anne Frank, *Diary of a Young Girl*

DREAMS OF GLORY

Pretend you are successful in a field of your choice or have achieved something important. You are being interviewed on TV or radio or for a magazine article. Write out the entire interview including a description of your achievement.

Write a newspaper story about your successful achievement. Be very specific. Write headlines to the article. Include who, what, where, when, and how. Give your name, age, where you live, who you are (i.e., student at X school), and what you achieved.

Draw a picture of yourself as an illustration of the article about your achievement.

THE TIME MACHINE

Imagine you have been given a special machine. It looks like a space vehicle, but instead of taking you into other galaxies, it takes you into other times. You walk into this "time machine," close the door, and set the dial on the control panel for Five Years. Suddenly, you are five years into the future. Where are you? What do you look like? How do you feel? Write about it. Describe anything that strikes you about your future self. Where do you live and work? What are your hobbies? What sort of lifestyle do you lead?

Draw a picture of yourself five years in the future.

Now, turn the dial on your time machine to a different setting. This time select one year into the future. Go through a typical day in this future time. Imagine yourself getting up in the morning, getting dressed, going through the day and evening, going to sleep at night. Describe where you are and what you do.

Draw a picture of yourself one year in the future.

Repeat this exercise as often as you like. Choose how far into the future to set your time machine.

I WISH

Write a story about yourself in which you meet someone who grants you three wishes. How and where do you meet this character? What does the character say to you? What do you wish for?

What happens after you get your wishes? How does it change your life? Be specific. Are you glad you made the wish you did? If not, why? Write about it.

Think about all the things you wish for: things to do, to see, to change, to enjoy, to create. Write a poem called "I Wish."

My Three Wishes

1. To be beautiful.
2. To have a family and a job.
3. To have a house full of love.

I Wish

I was in my car driving, when I just opened my mouth and said, "I wish I was rich and successful in a good job." Also I said, "I wish I had a great family." When I got home it was bedtime.

When I woke up the next morning I was in a different house with different people. Then this lady walks in the room, says, "Hi, Honey," and gives me a kiss. I was surprised about all this. When I got up to go to work, I had a selection of cars I could drive. Before I walked out to my car, I asked where I worked. My maid said I owned a business.

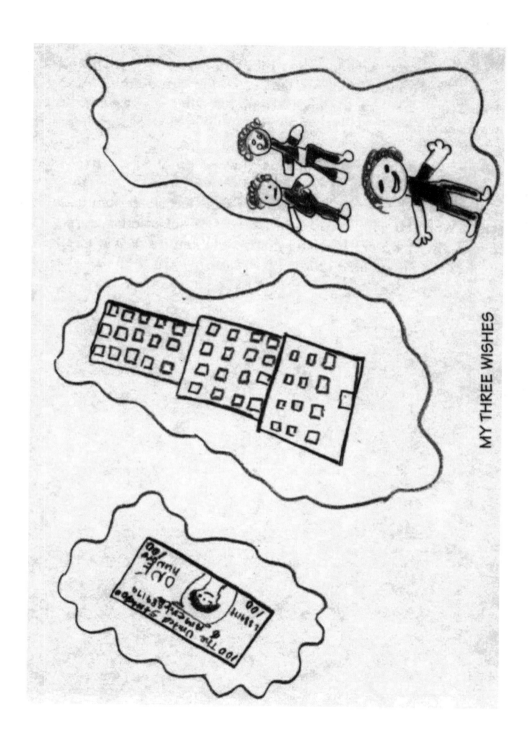

MY THREE WISHES

DREAM HOUSE

You have been on a TV show where you have won first prize: your own dream house. You get to design it and have it built wherever you want it—any place in the world. Close your eyes and picture it in your mind. What does it look like? Where is it?

Draw a floor plan of your dream house, including the outside area immediately surrounding it. Label the rooms or spaces.

Write a description of your dream house, its location, style or architecture, the rooms and other spaces, inside and outside.

Who lives in your dream house? Are you there alone? Are others living there with you? If so, who?

WHAT DO YOU WANT TO BE WHEN YOU GROW UP?

Almost all children imagine what they want to be when they grow up. Sometimes they act it but in make-believe games with hats and costumes and little dramas that they create.

Go back in your own memory of childhood and recall all the things you wanted to be "when you grew up." Put the pen in your "other hand" (the one you don't normally write with) and print—as if you were a child—all those dreams you used to have.

Now make a new list of things you'd like to be when you are an adult. Again, continue writing with your "other" (non-dominant) hand.

THE WINGS OF DREAMS

The poet Langston Hughes once wrote:

> "Hold fast to dreams,
>   for if dreams die,
>   life is a broken winged bird
>   that cannot fly."

What are *your* dreams? What are all the things you dream of doing, being, or experiencing in your lifetime? Write down your dreams. Be specific and describe each one as fully as possible.

Draw pictures about some of the dreams you wrote about.

One student wrote the following dreams:

When I get my degree in nursing, I would like to get married to the perfect man! And with that perfect man I want to start a family! And I want a house, or home, full of love and joy!

REWRITING MY LIFE

Think of a situation in your life that is uncomfortable, scary, or in some way unpleasant. Now re-create the situation by writing it the way you would like it to be. Change whatever you do not like into something positive.

Draw a picture of the biggest problem in your life at this time. Give the picture a title.

Now write about a conversation with the problem in your picture. Talk with your problem. Tell it what you want. Find out why it's there. What can you learn from having this problem?

Draw a picture of your solution to this problem. Really use your imagination.

CREATIVE DREAMING

When you wake up in the morning, do you remember your dreams? Think of a dream you've had. Draw a picture of any part or all of the dream. If there were several parts, draw it as a cartoon strip.

Write down what happened in the dream. Who said what? Who did what? Include how you felt in the dream and afterward.

Write down whatever thoughts come to mind about the dream. Don't "think" about it too much. Write quickly and freely.

Let the people or things that appeared in your dream "talk." Write out what each one says in the first person. For instance, "I'm the car in your dream. I ran away because my brake wasn't set...."

Think of a dream that had an unhappy ending or upset you in some way. Now rewrite the dream. Make it just the way you'd like it to be. Change all the parts you don't like so that it has an ending that you feel good about.

A BETTER WORLD

Make a list of world problems. If you can't think of any, here are some ideas: hunger, poverty, pollution, war, violence, disease, inadequate education, injustice, drug abuse, addictions.

You have suddenly been given the power to change anything in the world. Read your list of world problems. Write about the things you would change. Describe your plan. How would you go about changing things? Write down some ideas on how your list of changes could be brought about. Be specific.

Draw a picture of your solutions; for example, one student "invented" a machine that sucked in smog and turned it into rainbows.

Describe how things would be different after your "plan" of changes has been successfully put into effect.

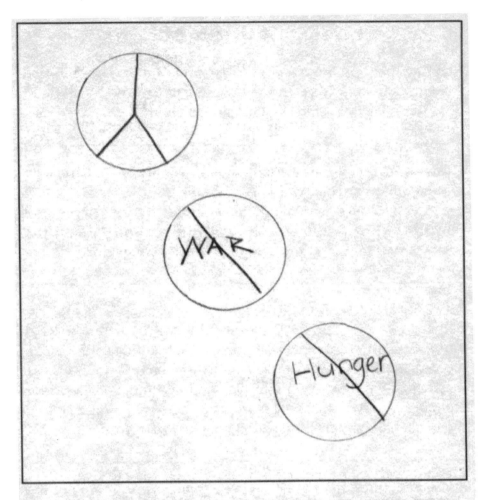

One day on my way to school, this old lady comes up to me and asks me if I had three wishes, what would they be. I said, "It's hard to wish just for three when there are a lot of things I want."

So I thought about it, and said, "I wish for peace among all human races, no more wars, and stop hunger all over." She looked at me, turned around, tapped her foot and said, "Here you go. All three come true." It was hard to believe everyone in the world was living better than just five minutes ago. But it was great and for generations to come everyone could live as one.

TREASURE MAP

Imagine that you are on a desert island searching for a buried treasure. In this case, the treasure is not money, jewels, or gold—it is your own hidden talents and abilities.

Draw a buried treasure map, showing your buried treasure and labeling it. Then draw in and label all the obstacles that get in your way. Draw in and label all the helpers (things and people) who assist you in getting to your goal: the development of your talents and abilities.

Think of a positive quality within yourself that is actually a helper to you in getting to your goal. Write down your goal and the quality that can assist you in reaching it. Then write a conversation between yourself and this positive quality. For instance, you might have a conversation with perseverance or courage. Tell why this goal is important to you. Will reaching the goal change your life? Will it change you? How?

Draw a picture of yourself having reached your goal. Let the you in the picture talk. Write down what it's like to have reached your goal.

Attitude: Why is graduation so important to you?

Me: Because I will be out of school and be able to get on with my life.

Att.: Why are you in such a hurry for that?

Me: Because I have more life after school than I do in school.

Att.: But why?

Me: Because people at school are just putting everyone down or putting on a show.

Att.: Why do you say that?

Me: People just think they have to be something they aren't.

Att.: Well what are you going to do after graduation?

Me.: I don't know. I just want to find a good job and live life to its fullest.

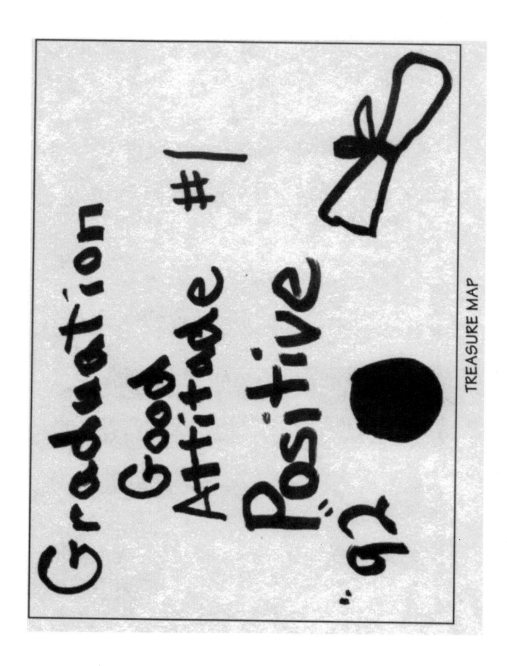

TREASURE MAP

CREATE YOUR OWN EXERCISE HERE

TITLE:

EXERCISE:

CREATE YOUR OWN EXERCISE HERE

TITLE:

EXERCISE:

Questions and Answers

I have gotten lots of questions about journaling
from teen readers and workshop participants.
This section has my answers to the kinds of questions that are most frequently asked. Hopefully
my comments will help you get more out of your
own Creative Journal.

*I have a hard time expressing my feelings. I've gotten laughed at or
put down when I got mad or sad about something. I don't know what
to do with these feelings. Sometimes I wish didn't have them. Would
keeping a journal help me with these emotions?*

Yes, journal drawing and writing would definitely help. First of
all, there is nothing wrong with any of your feelings. If people
are making fun of you or criticizing you, it's because *they* feel
uncomfortable. They were probably taught to judge those particular emotions. We need to accept *all* our feelings. That's what
journaling can help you do. Learn to *express* your feelings and
you'll learn to *accept* them, even if others don't.

The great thing about a journal is that you can be completely
honest with yourself. Nobody is going to laugh at you or put you
down. Journaling helps you accept your feelings and accept
yourself.

*I get very critical of myself when I write or draw in my journal.
I often think, Oh, this is an ugly drawing. Or I start finding mistakes in grammar or something. What can I do to be more
relaxed and just let it be?*

Heavy self-criticism is very stifling, as you have discovered. It
kills our creativity. Journaling is a great way to deal with self-
criticism because it's private. You're not writing or drawing for
anyone else's approval. You're not getting graded, and no one
else will criticize you. You just get to *be yourself.*

You also get to see how you treat yourself. So pat yourself on the
back for being so observant. Now that you see how you put yourself down, you can do something about it.

The Answering Back activity in Chapter Four is a great one to practice. As you keep journaling, just be aware of your critical self-talk (that voice in your own head that finds fault with you). But don't let it take control. Keep writing and drawing anyway. Have fun with your journal.

My emotions go out of control a lot, especially when I'm ticked off or frustrated. I try to hold the feelings in, but then they come bursting out. Would drawing or writing about these feelings in my journal help me?

Yes, a journal gives you a safe place to release strong feelings instead of blowing up. Drawing is especially helpful with anger and frustration. Just scribbling the emotion gets it off your chest. There's nothing wrong with feeling angry or frustrated, but you need to express it in a safe way. The journal is a great place to dump your feelings out—all of them.

Strong emotions are energy. That energy either goes out or stays bottled up inside. If we stuff our emotions or try not to feel them, they can cause health problems, such as tension headaches, stomach aches, or other illness. If we don't take charge of how to express our feelings, they can take charge of us. For example, they might eventually explode in destructive behavior. You can take charge of your emotions by choosing how and when to express them. If the emotions get really strong, just try writing about them with your dominant hand. Make friends with your emotions, and then they won't be so scary or powerful.

Another book that helps you take charge is *Living With Feeling: The Art of Emotional Expression.* In that book I show you how to use clay, painting, movement, and music to express emotions safely. The more creative ways you have to get your feelings out, the easier it is to live with them. Sports, dance, drama, singing, and dancing are also great ways to release strong emotions, so I'd recommend you consider those kinds of activities as well.

Caution: If your emotions are so out of control that you are hurting yourself, others, or the environment, then you really need to seek some sort of counseling or professional help. Perhaps there is a counselor at your school or another professional who can guide you. The Creative Journal method is not a substitute for therapy or counseling if you need it.

The drawing in this book is really fun and I even like the writing. It's funny because my grades in English aren't so great. English is my second language. Would keeping this kind of journal help me with my English classes? And would the drawing help me write better?

There's a very good chance it will. In a research project I directed the Creative Journal method was used with all the pupils in two southern California schools for a year. Reading and math scores in these schools went up as much as 20 percentile points that year. This district had mostly Hispanic and Asian students from homes where English was the second language, and all the testing was done in English.

First of all, practicing writing just for the fun of it is the best way to master written language skills. With journaling you're writing about what you know—yourself—and you're doing it without the fear of being graded. Those are excellent conditions for learning to write and to express yourself with words.

Secondly, there is an accepted method of teaching called the "language experience approach" that has proven very effective. This method uses art followed by language. The student creates a picture of an experience and then writes about it. That's what you are doing in many of these Creative Journal activities. So, yes, drawing can help with your writing skills because your drawing lets you see what you are writing about.

I notice that you don't stress grammar and spelling in your method of journaling. Why is that?

That's a good question. The reason is that I want you to relax and just practice putting your thoughts and feelings onto paper. If you have something interesting to write about, something you care about (such as your own life) you are more likely to write. The more you write, the better you'll get at it.

I have found that getting graded all the time makes students tense and anxious, especially those who are having trouble in school. It's important to have a place to apply what you learn without getting graded or having to take a test all the time.

Grammar, spelling, and syntax are what the schools teach you. However, first you have to *want* to learn those things. If you find you have something to say and want others to read it, you'll be more motivated to learn to write well. That will carry over into your classes. Some teens who have kept a Creative Journal discover, to their own surprise, that they actually have a talent for writing. They have gone on to write short stories or articles for their school papers

Since I got to high school, my grades have gotten pretty bad. My English teacher uses your book and I'm doing better in his class since we started the journals. Will journaling help me with my other classes, too?

Yes, it most probably will. Instruction and tests in American schools are in English. The more practice you get *writing* in English, the more likely you are to improve in school. You'll understand instruction better, in all your classes, and be able to do better on written tests.

Some of the students whose writing and drawings appear in this book were having a hard time in school, too. Some of them had the same challenge you do of having to learn English as a second language. Can you imagine how pleased these students were to be published? Their teacher told me that Creative Journaling helped them a lot, with English but also with self-confidence.

We're from another country and English is a second language for me. I'm doing OK in the classroom because I speak English well, but I'm not so good with written assignments and tests. Should I keep my journal in English?

You can keep a Creative Journal in any language you want. However, if you want to improve your writing skills for school, I'd recommend doing all or most of your journal work in English. After you have become proficient in written English then you can decide which language you want to use for personal journaling. Some bilingual people use two languages in their journals. One girl told me she wrote poetry and songs in Spanish and everything else in English. Also, her nondominant hand always wrote in Spanish.

I'm fifteen and my parents split up last year. When they argue about my weekend visits to my dad's house, I feel like I'm caught in the middle. Lots of times I feel like the divorce is my fault. Can

keeping a journal help me with all the feelings that come up?

Yes, it definitely can. But first you need to be clear on something: You are not responsible for the divorce. That was a choice your parents made. It is not your fault that their marriage did not work out. But you do have lots of *feelings* about the divorce and about the current situation. Those feelings are normal and to be expected. It's OK to have these feelings.

We are each responsible for our own feelings and choices. That's where the journal comes in. It's a place to express emotions in a safe place. Sometimes you may just want to scribble them out. At other times, the feelings may have words. Many kids tell me that their journal really helped them through similar situations to what you are going through.

Expressing emotions in your journal will help you understand yourself better. Anything that helps you understand yourself, can help you understand others as well. Write your needs in your journal, too. And then tell your parents what you need. They may not be able to fill all your needs, but it is important for you to tell them.

I go to a woman therapist as part of family therapy. Would your journal method help me with some of my problems with my family?

Journal-keeping is recommended by many therapists. Show *The Creative Journal for Teens* to your therapist and see what she thinks about using it along with your therapy. This book is being used in many schools and treatment centers, so she may already be familiar with it. Many therapists have their clients do journaling between sessions, and they often assign specific journal activities from this book.

I'm seventeen and in a 12-step recovery program for drug abuse. Would keeping a Creative Journal help me with my recovery?

Yes, journaling is a great tool to use in combination with any recovery program. Many addictions counselors are recommending my method for that purpose, especially for doing personal inventories. And I have gotten lots of mail from readers in recovery who have gotten a lot out of this book. You may want to discuss this book with your sponsor and any counselor you are seeing as part of your recovery.

Addictions are a way to numb feelings that are too painful. The feelings don't go away. They just go underground. In recovery, the feelings that were pushed down start to surface. Creative Journaling helps you get in touch with your true feelings. It also gives you a place to express them safely.

After you've kept a journal for a while, you can use my book *Recovery of Your Inner Child,* a program for reparenting yourself. It is being used in recovery programs and in centers for addictions counseling. It teaches you how to nurture and protect yourself and take care of the emotional part of you.

After going through the material in that book, you can graduate to another book of mine entitled *Living with Feeling: The Art of Emotional Expression.* This books gives you a complete program for expressing emotions safely through art, movement, music, and so on. You don't need any talent in the arts to do any of these activities, either.

I've been taking private art classes all through high school and I'd like to have a career in graphic design. Would drawing in my journal help me develop more skill?

Yes, many people who have used my Creative Journal method have gone on to become professional artists or art teachers. One of the reasons this method is so great for developing talent is that you can write about the obstacles you face, such as self-criticism or lack of confidence. Every artist has to deal with that. As you progress with journal work, you can graduate to my book *The Power of Your Other Hand,* which was written for adults but has been used by some teens. It shows you how to deal with self-doubt and inner criticism.

In addition to drawing, writing in the journal will help with your career. The more you express yourself in words, the better prepared you will be to go out into the job market when the time comes. Employers don't hire artwork, they hire a person: you. And you need to be able to communicate with people on the job.

If you want to develop your talent, I'd recommend another book of mine, *Putting Your Talent to Work.* This book can really help you get your career off the ground. I co-authored it with Peggy Van Pelt, a longtime Disney artist and talent development coordinator. She has years of experience working with top talent in the Disney organization and is one of the country's leading experts on creativity in the workplace. She and I worked together at Walt Disney Imagineering (designers of the theme parks) where I was a consultant for ten years.

My mother gave me activities from your book, The Creative Journal for Children, *when I was a kid. Now that I'm sixteen and using* The Creative Journal for Teens, *I've gotten interested in a career in art therapy. Have you written any books on the subject?*

Yes, I've written many books that apply art therapy techniques. I'd suggest you start with my first book, *The Creative Journal: The Art of Finding Yourself.* It has been used for years as a textbook in art therapy graduate programs. Because you are a veteran of my method, I think you are ready for that book even though it was written for adults.

After that, you might want to read *The Picture of Health: Healing Your Life with Art.* It explains how art works as therapy and has lots of activities as well as some wonderful examples from people's journals.

Living with Feeling: The Art of Emotional Expression would be another valuable book for you. That book is about a new field called expressive arts therapy. It goes beyond art therapy and shows how all the arts can be combined (music, drama, dance, writing, and art) and used therapeutically. Expressive arts therapy is one of the newer career choices for people interested in art for healing.

I've been drawing and writing using The Creative Journal for Teens *for about a year and I love my journal. I just got your book,* Visioning, *and started using that to make photo collages of what I want in my life. When doing some of the drawing activities in* The Creative Journal for Teens *could I include snapshots and magazine photos?*

Yes, collages are a great way to do these journal assignments. However, I wouldn't want to see you drop drawing and writing altogether, because these forms of expression bring out a different set of abilities. Why not try *combining* collage and drawing, as well? Decorate your pages with colors, lines, and patterns along with the photo images.

I edit the school paper and I really like journalism. I want to be a writer or a journalist. Would keeping a Creative Journal help me toward a writing career?

I've met lots of journalists who keep a personal journal. They tell me that's how they got in the habit of writing, and how they developed their skills, too. That was certainly true for me. I hadn't intended to become a writer when I started keeping a journal; it just happened naturally. After spending so much time with my journal, writing came automatically. After a few years I started writing my first book. If you are serious about becoming a journalist, my book *Putting Your Talent to Work* could really help.

Many people have become professional writers after using my journal method. Writing isn't a full-time livelihood for all of them, but quite a few have published stories or even books. One has written a screenplay that was produced as a Hollywood film. Others have written autobiographical short stories, plays, and even television shows.

I plan to go into nursing, but my teachers tell me I have talent in writing. Writing is fun, but I don't want to become a writer for a career. Would keeping a journal be a good hobby for me to pursue?

I never thought of journaling as a hobby, but why not? You're not getting grades for journal-keeping, so you can relax and do this for fun. And because it is personal, you don't have to show it to anyone, so there's no pressure to perform. You're just writing for yourself. So, sure, you can think of it as a hobby.

Sometimes I write things in my journal that I'd like to develop and show to others. Like some poems I wrote and some pages that could become a short story. I'd have to copy them out and edit them or polish them up. Is it OK to do that?

Yes, that's a great thing to do. Many writers use their personal journal as a place to get ideas for their *public* writing (meaning pieces that they share with others or actually publish). Just don't do your journal writing with this as your goal. Otherwise you'll start editing and correcting and polishing your journal work and the honesty and spontaneity will go out of it.

If you find you have a talent in writing, consider taking creative writing classes or writer's workshops. That's a place to work on your writing skills and share what you write with others. If you do get into a class or group, be sure it's a safe place. You don't need negative criticism or to feel put down. Rather, you want support, encouragement, and the inspiration you get from good writing done by others.

I've written some things in my journal that I think would make good short stories for my English class. Is it all right to do that, or should journal writing just stay private?

It's true that the journal needs to be kept private because you don't want to be worrying about making technical errors or about getting the approval of others. You want to be free to be honest with yourself. However, taking materials or ideas out of the journal and developing them for school assignments is an excellent idea. You might even want to tell your teacher that the original ideas for your paper came from your journal.

Will keeping a Creative Journal make me more creative?

Yes, if you stick with it. The journal is a fantastic place to develop creativity and talent in art, writing, and other areas of life. Judging from letters I've received, this method seems to encourage observational skills, self-reflection, and creative problem-solving. You can eventually apply what you learn from journaling to all areas of your life and career.

Many famous leaders in the arts, science, and religion kept journals, notebooks, or diaries. Their initial ideas formed in their personal writings. Later they worked on those ideas and created plays, essays, novels, nonfiction books, inventions, geographical explorations, and more. Some famous journals were so well-written they were eventually published, such as the diary of Anne Frank.

As for myself, I never intended to publish anything from my journal. However, some of my journal drawings have been the basis for paintings and other art work I eventually exhibited. And all of my books and classes started with ideas I first jotted down in my journals.

I'm really into computers and am thinking about becoming a graphic designer. Could I do Creative Journal activities on the computer?

Yes, there are many activities that could be done this way. You can also scan in some images and do your own collages on the computer.

Actually, I suggest doing both computer art and handmade art. And here's why: Drawing or scribbling with crayons or felt pens on paper is superior to computer graphics for releasing strong emotions. With simple art materials, such as the ones you used in kindergarten, you can be more spontaneous and more physical, too. You really get the feelings out and let off some steam. There's nothing like scribbling with crayons. The activities that require using the nondominant hand should also be done by hand, not on a computer.

When I did the journal exercise where I used my left hand (I'm right-handed), a lot of really strong feelings came up. At first I got frustrated because it was so slow and awkward. Then I got mad and started talking back to the critical voice in my head, the way you said to do. Then I started laughing and feeling silly. Is that what usually happens?

Yes, it is common for people to feel all sorts of emotions when they use their nondominant hand. It seems to tap into parts of the brain that govern our ability to express feelings. So emotions may come out more easily through that hand. Most people tell me how relieved they feel after doing the activity of answering back. It sounds as if you did, too.

In that assignment where we write with the nondominant hand, I wasn't sure which hand to use. I throw a ball and use a hammer with my left hand, but I write and use scissors with my right hand. Which is my nondominant hand?

For our purposes here, the nondominant hand is the one you *don't normally write with*. It doesn't matter which hand you use for other activities. Just use the opposite hand to the one you usually write with.

I got really frustrated writing with my other hand. It is so slow and awkward. I'm right-handed and my right hand wanted to grab the pen away from my left hand and take over. Do other people have that reaction?

That happens all the time in workshops. Writing with the non-dominant hand is frustrating for most people. That hand wasn't taught to write, so it is awkward. This kind of writing forces you to slow down. That's hard to do when you've been taught to hurry up. At school you're graded on how quickly you can complete a test or assignment. And lots of other activities, such as sports and games, are based on the fastest one being the winner.

By contrast, journaling is about slowing down and thinking about your life and yourself. There's no rush here. You are not being graded or compared to anyone else. There are no deadlines to meet.

I'm usually a pretty good speller, but when I wrote with the hand I don't usually write with, I made some really dumb mistakes in spelling. It was like a little kid was writing. Does that happen a lot?

Yes, actually it happens to both adults and teens. It even happens to me. And, like you, I've always been good at spelling. When you write with the nondominant hand, you are tapping into parts of the brain that help us express emotions, orient ourselves to our environment, make art or listen to our hunches. Those areas of the brain are *not* designed for language skills, so it makes sense that spelling and grammar won't come as easily when you're in that part of your brain.

The best part of this book was when I talked back to the critical things I say to myself. I got really mad and sassed back. And then I just started laughing. That was great! Do people usually feel that way after doing that exercise?

Yes, they do. I've conducted hundreds of workshops that included this technique. It never fails. People start laughing and giggling when they have really answered back to that critic that lives in their head. They talk about what a relief it was.

I'm nervous about people in my family reading my journal. What can I do to prevent that from happening?

This is probably the hardest question for me to answer. Each situation is so different. But there are some general precautions you can take.

First of all, keep your journal in a private place. **Do not leave it around for anyone to just pick up and browse through**. Some teens are in a similar situation to yours. They tell me they keep their journals in the back of a dresser drawer wrapped in clothing or tucked away in a storage box in their closet. Some use a box with a lock and key designed for storing important papers.

In addition to those precautions, other teens report that they put a label on the cover of their journals saying, "Private. Do not open." (or something similar). But they also keep their journal in a safe place.

Some journal-keepers feel safe about letting family members know that they keep a personal journal. However, they also make it clear that their journal is private. And they don't leave it lying around for anybody to just pick up and look at.

Unfortunately, not all people respect the privacy of others. If privacy is a serious problem in your household, then you may need to take other precautions. If you think other family members are likely to pry into your journal, then keeping it in a safe place is really important.

One girl kept her journal in the safe-keeping of a friend whose family respected privacy. She put a "privacy" label on the cover and it was kept in a safe spot. A boy who was seeing a counselor kept his journal at the counselor's office because he was afraid that his siblings would try to read it. Be creative and figure out a way to safeguard your journal.

Sometimes I share things I've drawn or written in my journal with my best friend. Is that OK, or should I keep everything to myself?

If your friend is trustworthy, then there's nothing wrong with sharing certain parts of your journal. The same is true with anyone in your life. If you trust the person then it is usually fine to share certain portions of your journal work.

When I say trust, I mean that the person will keep it confidential. You need to be sure that he or she isn't going to tell anybody else what you shared. It's nobody else's business but yours and the person you share it with. Use common sense and be careful whenever you show anything from your journal with someone. Be sure to tell the person beforehand that you don't want this discussed with anyone else. If they can't keep it confidential, then don't share it.

Trust also includes feeling emotionally safe with the person. Safe means that they don't judge you or put you down. You don't need anyone criticizing how you write or draw in your journal. Remember, this is not about performing for others. It's about getting to know yourself. If sharing with people who are safe helps, then feel free to share.

I have an English teacher that I really like. I'd like to share some of my journal pages with him. Would that be an OK thing to do?

Read the answer to the previous question and follow those guidelines. If your teacher is trustworthy, safe, and will respect your privacy, then it should be OK First tell him that this is confidential. If he has a problem with that, then it's best not to share. Also, I'd ask the teacher how he feels about you sharing certain portions of your journal with him. He may think it's fine, or he may have some reason why he wouldn't want you to share it.

Now that I've been keeping a journal for a couple of years, I like myself much better. My best friend is always putting herself down. I think journaling would really help her. What can I do to convince her?

Instead of trying to convince her of anything, just be honest and tell her what you've gotten out of journaling. If she knows you and has seen the changes, she may just want to try it. Don't push it, because then she might feel pressured and get turned off. Just tell her how you feel about the changes in yourself. Then let your actions speak louder than your words.

My aunt gave me your book last year and since I started keeping a Creative Journal I feel like a different person. I'm doing better in school and I'm getting clear about what I want to do when I graduate. I think your book should be required reading for all high school students. How can I get my teachers interested in using this with other kids?

Just be honest and tell them what journaling has meant to you. If they have noticed your improvement at school, they may be eager to hear the reasons. Just share your experiences and let them draw their own conclusions.

I'm in homeschooling and my sisters and I have been using your journal books for a few years. I'm only sixteen, but was wondering if I was ready for some of your other books. I know they are written for adults, so wasn't sure it was right for me. What do you think?

Many teenagers who started with my books for children and teens graduate to my other books and do quite well with them. A lot depends on your own interests. The books that teens seem to gravitate toward are *The Creative Journal: The Art of Finding Yourself, Putting Your Talent to Work,* and *Visioning: Ten Steps to Designing the Life of Your Dreams.* I'd suggest going to a bookstore and looking through those books to see which one interests you most. Start there.

I was always so worried about what others thought of me. Now that I've been journaling for a few months, what others think about me isn't so important. There are some kids who I used to hang out with that I just don't enjoy anymore. They're into drinking and stuff that I don't want to be part of. Does that mean I am getting antisocial or something?

Not at all. It sounds like you're just setting new priorities for yourself. In adolescence it is normal to be influenced by your peer group. By forming ties with non-family members in your own age group, you start the process of eventually creating a life of your own. Any circle of friends is like a new family. Sometimes, what a teen's friends think may seem more important than what the teen thinks or what his family thinks.

The danger for teens is that they are sometimes controlled by peer group pressure. They will do anything to be liked and accepted by the group. For example, if their friends are into drugs, they will join in, whether they really want to or not. Anything to be popular. Fortunately, it sounds as if you are freeing yourself from the need to conform to the group. You didn't like what those kids were doing, so you dropped them.

Eventually, you will need to create a life that works for you. Journaling can help you find your own values, set your priorities and make choices based on who you are and what's important to you. That includes figuring out what kind of friends you want. Use your journal as the place to design the life you want, including the kinds of friendships. You might want to use my book *Visioning: Ten Steps to Designing the Life of Your Dreams* and do some collages. Picture what kinds of things you'd be doing with your new friends. Really give it some thought. It's up to you to create your family of friends.

I'm sixteen and am a few months pregnant. A counselor I'm seeing suggested this book, so I started keeping a Creative Journal. It's real helpful because I've been dealing with a lot of difficult feelings. Do you have any books about parenting using this method?

Yes, my book *The Creative Journal for Parents* would be the book to use right now. I've created journal activities to do during the period of pregnancy and birth, then on to parenting an infant and going all the way to raising an adolescent. It's a book that can accompany you through the whole adventure of being a parent. There are also chapters on single-parenting, blended families, adoption, and a broad range of parenting situations.

I am obese and have an eating disorder. I'm in counseling with a woman who specializes in these issues. She has me keeping a journal. Do you have any journal books that would be suitable for me?

Yes, *Lighten Up Your Body, Lighten Up Your Life* has journal activities designed to help people who are facing such challenges. It presents drawing and writing exercises that help the reader reflect on attitudes and beliefs about the body, about food, and other issues related to weight, body image, and eating disorders. I'd suggest that you discuss the book with your counselor to see if it would fit in with what she is doing with you.

My brother committed suicide a few years ago. I don't seem to be able to get over it. Every time I think about him, so many feelings come up. Sometimes I just get so mad that he did it. Other times I feel so sad and depressed that I don't want to do anything but cry. Putting my feelings in my journal helps, but then more feelings come up a few days later. What can I do?

The journal is a good place to express these feelings. You will probably always have feelings about your brother's death. Grieving doesn't just run its course and end one day. When you think you've cried all the tears you have, something may remind you of your brother and more feelings will come up.

If your grief feels overwhelming and makes it hard for you to concentrate or carry out your daily tasks, you might want to get some help. There are therapists and support groups for dealing specifically with grief. Many communities offer free grief counseling programs and support groups run by volunteers. Talk to your family about this.

Every time I see another news show about kids shooting and killing other kids in schools, I get freaked out. It's gotten so that I am afraid to go to school. We live in a nice neighborhood, but that doesn't seem to matter anymore. Some of the worst cases of this have been in really affluent areas. Can journaling help me with these feelings?

It can. Anything that lets you express these feelings will help. But if you are so filled with fear that you don't want to go to school, I think you need to talk to someone about it as well: a trusted family member or a counselor. Someone who won't laugh at you or try to talk you out of these feelings.

It is perfectly understandable that you would feel anxious considering all the terrible tragedies in our nation in recent years. I feel very upset about the increasing violence I see in schools and in our nation. I don't have to go to school every day, but you do. And my heart goes out to you, and all the kids like you, who have to face the possibility of violence at school.

It is my hope that your generation and mine can work together to stop this trend, but in order to do it we need to communicate. Tell people you trust how you feel. They can't make your feelings go away, but they can listen. And you can honor your true feelings, in your journal and in your relationships with others. I believe you will be the stronger for it.

My boyfriend and I are always arguing. I've tried to break up with him, but I'm afraid of being alone. I just started keeping a journal in my English class. Would your method help me figure things out?

I believe it would. You already realize that you are afraid of being alone. That's great. To be aware of that at a young age is a great advantage. Many people don't figure that out until late in life, but they've put up with a bad situation for years because of fear of loneliness. Keeping a journal can give you the inner strength to be alone and to enjoy being with yourself.

Most importantly, journal work can help you get clear on your priorities and preferences. What kind of life do you want? What kind of relationships do you want? Decide on that and then go for it. Don't settle for less when you don't have to.

I have lots of problems with headaches. My doctor thinks some of it might be emotional and he has encouraged me to get my feelings out. Can your method of journaling help me?

Yes, I think it could. I have a couple of books specifically for dealing with emotional expression as part of a wellness program. They are *The Picture of Health: Healing Your Life with Art* and *The Well-Being Journal*. Another book of mine that would help is *Living with Feeling: The Art of Emotional Expression*. I field tested both books with groups of people who were dealing with chronic stress, pain, and threatening illnesses. The results were very good. Show these books to your doctor and see what he or she thinks about using these techniques. You might also ask your doctor if some sort of counseling would be a advisable.

Dear Reader:

I recommend reading back over each volume of your journal when you complete it. Then write down your feelings and reactions to what you have read. This is an extremely valuable way to observe yourself and learn from your own experiences. Enjoy the adventure!

If you'd like to write to me about your journal experiences, please do. You can write to me at P.O. Box 5805, Santa Monica, CA 90409.

Best Wishes,
Lucia Capacchione

Recommended Reading

Diary of a Young Girl, by Anne Frank, Modem Library, 1952.

Linotte: The Early Diary of Anaïs Nin 1914-1920, by Anaïs Nin, Harcourt, Brace, Jovanovich, 1978.

The Creative Journal: The Art of Finding Yourself, by Lucia Capacchione, New Page Books, 2001.

The Creative Journal for Children, by Lucia Capacchione, Shambhala Publications, 1989.